IMAGES
of America

SACRAMENTO'S
ELMHURST, TAHOE PARK,
AND COLONIAL HEIGHTS

Looking southeast over the California State Fair and Exposition (bounded by V Street on the left, Stockton Boulevard on the right, and Broadway to the right of the racetrack), this c. 1927 aerial photograph foreshadows the suburban growth to come south and east of Sacramento. Elmhurst (to the left of the racetrack) has a few elm trees visible that would later become the neighborhood's signature. Elmhurst would eventually be cut off from the city by construction of Highway 50. The suburb of Tahoe Park (to the right of the racetrack) was the site of a housing boom after World War II. The new Sacramento County Hospital is shown in the foreground nearing completion. The original hospital is immediately behind the new buildings. Opening in 1909, the state fair eventually became landlocked by suburban growth, forcing city and state planners to begin searching for a new locale. The last fair at the Stockton Boulevard site would be in 1967. (Courtesy Sacramento Metropolitan Chamber of Commerce Collection.)

ON THE COVER: When built in 1910, developers of the Colonial Heights subdivision constructed a wide palm tree–lined thoroughfare into three separate lanes that they named San Francisco Boulevard. The street runs from Stockton Boulevard on the west to Fifty-seventh Street on the east. This photograph, taken in the spring of 1964, shows three boys enjoying a bicycle ride down the center lane. (Courtesy *Sacramento Bee* Collection.)

IMAGES
of America

SACRAMENTO'S
ELMHURST, TAHOE PARK,
AND COLONIAL HEIGHTS

Sacramento Archives
and Museum Collection Center

ARCADIA
PUBLISHING

Copyright © 2008 by Sacramento Archives and Museum Collection Center
ISBN 978-1-5316-3551-0

Published by Arcadia Publishing
Charleston SC, Chicago IL, Portsmouth NH, San Francisco CA

Library of Congress Catalog Card Number: 2007933017

For all general information contact Arcadia Publishing at:
Telephone 843-853-2070
Fax 843-853-0044
E-mail sales@arcadiapublishing.com
For customer service and orders:
Toll-Free 1-888-313-2665

Visit us on the Internet at www.arcadiapublishing.com

Taken nearly 65 years after the previous photograph, the former fairground region has changed dramatically. Stockton Boulevard is in the upper left with the campus of the University of California, Davis, Medical Center lining the east side of the street. The large area in the center was once the site of the California State Fair and Exposition. In this 1991 aerial, the grounds are now dotted with medical offices and state and county governmental buildings. Highway 50 is on the top, and just below it are the tree-lined streets of the Elmhurst neighborhood with its parklike setting along T Street. Broadway is in the lower foreground with the California State Department of Justice campus on the north side of the street. Tahoe Park and Colonial Heights neighborhoods are in the lower foreground. (Courtesy City of Sacramento Collection.)

CONTENTS

ACKNOWLEDGMENTS

The staff at the Sacramento Archives and Museum Collection Center (SAMCC) would like to thank all who supported us in the production of this book. It was through Sacramento City council member Kevin McCarty's efforts to promote the history of his district that this project was undertaken. Our thanks go to the people at Arcadia Publishing for their help and guidance, especially our editor, John T. Poultney.

We particularly want to thank the residents of Elmhurst, Tahoe Park, and Colonial Heights neighborhoods for the photographs they contributed to the Faces and Places of Sacramento neighborhood history project. The photographs we used from this project added a more personal touch to the book. Additionally, we would like to thank the volunteers who assisted in gathering those images at the Faces and Places of Sacramento event.

A huge debt of gratitude is owed to our volunteer photograph editor, Kevin Morse, who spent countless hours searching out not only great photographs to use in the book, but ferreting out information about them that proved extremely useful in telling the story of the neighborhood. Using records at SAMCC and the California State Library, particularly newspaper accounts, Kevin researched and checked the accuracy of our work.

We would especially like to thank the photographers and collectors who are the ultimate source of the over five million images in SAMCC's collections: Eugene Hepting, David Joslyn, the McCurry Foto Company, Ernest Myers, Michael Benning, Frank Christy, Harry Sweet, and all the others too numerous to mention. We could not have written this particular book without the *Sacramento Bee* photographers' collection and photograph morgue. Constituting the majority of images used in the depiction of this neighborhood account, the *Bee's* images were invaluable.

Thanks also go to Greg King and Deborah Dalton with the California Department of Transportation; Clare Ellis and Tom Tolley of the Sacramento Room, Sacramento Public Library; Amy Johnston and Nicole Townsend of Raley's; Julie Thomas at the CSUS Special Collections and University Archives; and Lois Dove.

INTRODUCTION

"Sacramento City," as it was first called, was laid out in a 4.5-square mile grid pattern and remained unchanged for 62 years. From the original city boundaries, the initial annexation was to the south and east and included the earliest suburbs of Oak Park and East Sacramento. With this first annexation in 1911, the city more than doubled in size. The Central California Traction Company opened an interurban line from the city's center out to the California State Fair grounds (which opened on Upper Stockton Road and Fifth Avenue in 1909) and the new neighborhoods of Elmhurst and Colonial Heights in 1910.

It would be another 35 years before any more annexations took place. At the close of World War II, new neighborhoods began springing up to house the workers and their families who remained in Sacramento after the war. The need for affordable housing would see the further development of Sacramento's Tahoe Park and the surrounding areas of Colonial Heights, or "The Heights," as they were also known. With the housing came schools, churches, and recreation. In addition, business and industry located in the region to provide employment for returning veterans and the resultant population boom. For the purposes of this book, the geographic boundaries discussed within are Stockton Boulevard on the west, Highway 50 to the north, Power Inn Road on the east, and Fruitridge Road on the south. The chapters on transportation and business further move the boundaries out to Florin-Perkins Road and Elder Creek Road.

Readers will recognize the thematic approach used in the organization of this book. The authors concentrated on the neighborhoods reflected in the title that define the region. These three chapters include the schools, churches, community centers, and other services to residents of the area. Today there are more than a dozen recognized neighborhood associations that assist residents with community issues. The Elmhurst subdivision, with its signature tree-lined streets, is the gateway to the three chapters on the residential developments. Tahoe Park includes West Tahoe Park and Tahoe Park East. The authors made the determination that the region south of Fourteenth Avenue would be included in the Colonial Heights chapter. In addition to the original tract laid out in 1910, "The Colonials" would also encompass Colonial Acres, Colonial Manor, and Colonial Village. As the Tallac Village tracts are adjacent to the Colonials, they are included with their Colonial Heights neighbors.

The remaining four chapters focus on business and industry, transportation issues, the Sacramento County Hospital, and the California State Fair. Chapter four discusses the business corridors, shopping centers, and industries that provided employment and services to the residents such as the Coca Cola Bottling Company, Fruitridge Manor Shopping Center, the Proctor and Gamble Manufacturing Company, and the U.S. Army Depot. Chapter five is devoted to the various forms of transportation in the region. Starting with the electric streetcars that ran out to the fairgrounds and into the new Colonial Heights tract, these new forms would give way to the automobile and the problems of access into the neighborhood. The city would construct new roads, widen them, and then change the routes all in an effort to relieve the congestion. Chapter six focused on the evolution of health care in Sacramento from the construction of the first county hospital on

Upper Stockton Road to the state-of-the-art University of California, Davis teaching hospital of today. Lastly, chapter seven provides a brief overview of the state fair. It recounts the roots of the institution, its struggle to locate permanently in Sacramento, and ultimately its history at the Stockton Boulevard site.

The Sacramento Archives and Museum Collection Center (SAMCC) grew out of the early Landmarks Commission. This organization was responsible for the core collections that developed into what the archives is today. The Landmarks Commission evolved into the Sacramento Museum and History Commission responsible for developing a museum for Sacramento. As a result, collections began to grow, with the largest expansion between 1977 and 1983. During that time, the Sacramento Museum and History Commission became an official division of Sacramento city government, creating the official archives.

One

ELMHURST

BY REBECCA CARRUTHERS
AND PATRICIA J. JOHNSON

The area southeast of Sacramento's original city boundaries was farm and ranch lands. While the suburb of Fruit Vale was platted by county surveyor John C. Boyd in 1892 for the purpose of "fine suburban homes with twenty to forty fruit trees on each lot," the subdivision was never built. The property remained farmland until 1908 when H. A. McClelland acquired nearly 250 acres or the equivalent of 80 city blocks from the original owners, Williamson, Oats, and Odbert for the purpose of laying out the new subdivision he called Elmhurst. Elm trees became the signature for the area as McClelland planted the trees, installed the curbs and sidewalks, and required that barns and power lines be on the back of the lots in the alleys. The *Sacramento Union* newspaper reported in June 1911 that the improvements in the new subdivision "are fast transforming it into [an] ideal residence section." The city annexed this area and the other nearby subdivisions in 1911. (Courtesy Joan Dangermond Collection.)

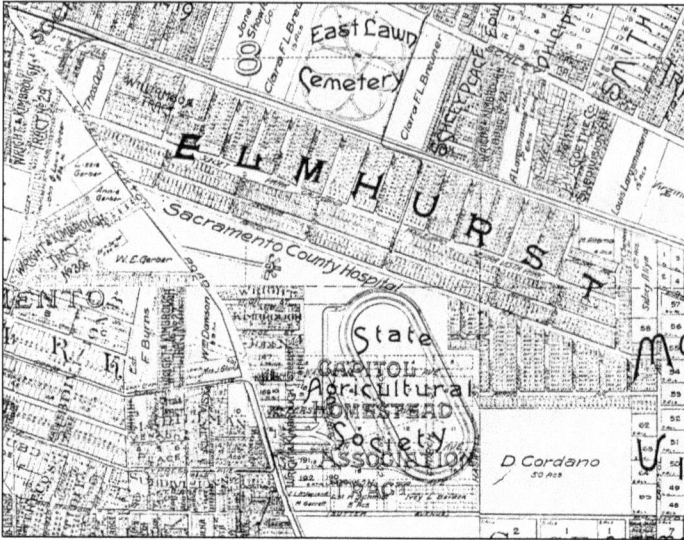

This 1913 area map shows the property east of Stockton Boulevard and south of the Southern Pacific Railroad line now established as the new suburb of Elmhurst. Note that Sunset Park and Sierra Vista Park still exist in the neighborhood along California Boulevard. In 1916, the city standardized street names in the new annexed area, changing California Boulevard to the now very scenic tree-lined T Street. (Courtesy City of Sacramento Collection.)

This is the southwest corner of Stockton Boulevard and Miller Way as it appeared in 1933 just before the building of the new Coca Cola Bottling Company plant in 1936. The Anne Gerber family farm is seen in the background. The buildings would be demolished to make way for the bottling plant. Gerber Way intersects with Stockton Boulevard just on the edge of Elmhurst. (Courtesy Bob McCabe Collection.)

This view of Forty-first Street and Stockton Boulevard looks northwest at the Anne Gerber family farm on the left as it appeared in November 1939. The new Coca Cola Bottling Company plant, which opened in 1936, is in the background at Miller Way and Stockton Boulevard just on the edge of Elmhurst. (Courtesy Eugene Hepting Collection.)

The new Coca Cola Bottling Company plant is under construction in this view from 1936. Seen at the corner of Stockton Boulevard and Miller Way, Anne Gerber's family residence is in the rear. The Gerber homestead would be sold to the Carmelite Sisters for their monastery that they occupied until they built their new brick building in 1954. (Courtesy Eugene Hepting Collection.)

This 1940s ragtag boy's baseball team poses with their uniforms, provided by local sponsor Keystone Market. The corner market was located at Stockton Boulevard and T Streets. Typical of most municipal parks and recreation departments, leagues obtained sponsors for uniforms and equipment. Having the business logo on the shirts was another mode of advertising. (Courtesy Sacramento Parks and Recreation Department Collection.)

A crew of workers poses in front of Pacific Telephone and Telegraph Company's new office, South Dial at 2216 Stockton Boulevard, in 1942. The telephone company was just across the street from the old state fairgrounds. Pictured from left to right are Stan Mills, Earl Kirtland, Ben Northup, Nick Athey, Al Green, Dave Joslyn, and Bill Young. (Courtesy David Joslyn Collection.)

The Born brothers, George and William, operated the Harelson Feed Company business on Stockton Boulevard between S and T Streets from 1880 until a devastating fire destroyed the buildings in 1943. While the brothers' feed store sold supplies to local farmers and ranchers, they also operated a grocery business at Eighth and M Street. This view is from December 25, 1938. (Courtesy Eugene Hepting Collection.)

"Access Sacramento" radio station KCBL, as it was first called, began operating their broadcasting studio at 4673 T Street in 1986. The station today is now nicknamed "The Voice" and is still on T Street at the Coloma Community Center. It is a free-form cable radio station that invites the community to bring in their music and information to share on a weekly basis. (Courtesy *Suttertown News* Collection.)

Elmhurst Methodist Church, under the leadership of the Reverend Albert E. Raugust, began serving its congregants in 1951. Located at 1801 Fifty-first Street in Elmhurst, the sanctuary building of the church seen here was brand new when this picture was taken in August 1951. (Courtesy Frank Christy Collection.)

Into the 1960s, the Elmhurst Methodist Church continued to thrive and expand. The congregation added a Sunday school building at 1827 Fifty-first Street and the Reverend Chester W. McCaskey served as pastor. In this exterior view, an unidentified couple poses amid the shrubbery that has grown up around the sanctuary. (Courtesy McCurry Company Collection.)

Members of the Third Ward of the Church of Jesus Christ of Latter-day Saints, or the Mormon Church as it is commonly called, worshiped in Elmhurst at 4647 U Street. Built in 1932, the Mission Revival–style building served the church until the late 1970s when the Capital City Masonic Temple Association took over the site, which they still occupy today. (Courtesy Ralph Shaw Collection.)

The Carmelite Sisters established their new monastery on the old Anne Gerber farm property at 2110 Stockton Boulevard in 1954 on the edge of Elmhurst. This view of the building is just after they completed the work. Originally the Sisters purchased the property from Miss Gerber in 1935. The Carmelites occupied the old Gerber farmhouse for nearly 20 years before they built the new monastery. (Courtesy *Catholic Herald* Collection.)

Upon completion of the monastery in 1954, the Sisters invited the faithful to tour the new sanctuary. Congregants gathered for baptisms and other church ceremonies. After 25 years at the Stockton Boulevard location, the Sisters relocated the monastery in 1979 due to changes in the neighborhood. The Carmelites moved to Georgetown in 1982, where they still administer the monastery. (Courtesy *Catholic Herald* Collection.)

Faith Bible Church at Fifty-ninth and U Streets in Elmhurst is an affiliated member of the nondenominational Independent Fundamental Churches of America, International. Pastor Herbert M. Fox organized the church in 1947. They laid the foundation in 1948, and the men of the congregation worked many weekends and holidays to complete the building. The dedication was Sunday, July 30, 1950, and the church is still ministering to its congregation today. (Courtesy *Sacramento Bee* Collection.)

16

Giacomo "Jim" and Carolina Dallosta moved to this house at 3665 T Street about 1915. In 1921, they built a cottage on the rear of the property. It can be seen at right in the background. The home and outbuilding were torn down in 1958 to make way for the telephone company. Their son Carlo is on the step in the foreground. Carolina is on the second-floor balcony. (Courtesy Dolores Dallosta Collection.)

The Dallostas lived in their home on T Street for over 40 years. Jim and Carolina are seen sitting at their dining room table. Jim worked for the City of Sacramento laying sewer and gas pipes. He also owned a bar and restaurant at 610 J Street next to the Ramona Hotel called the Zero Inn. Later his son Carlo took over the bar and changed the name to the Argentina. (Courtesy Dolores Dallosta Collection.)

The Julia Morgan House at 3731 T Street was built for Sacramento businessman Charles M. Goethe and his wife, Mary Glide, in the 1920s. Morgan, best known for Randolph Hearst's Castle in San Simeon, was the architect. In 1966, Goethe bequeathed the house to California State University, Sacramento, an institution he helped establish. The house was placed on the National Register of Historic Places in 1982. (Courtesy Charles M. Goethe papers, CSUS Special Collections and University Archives.)

Julius S. Gattmann built the house at 3821 T Street in 1913 and lived there until 1921 when he sold the house to Dr. Gustave Wilson, a physician and surgeon. Gattmann was in partnership with David S. Wasserman, and they operated the Nonpareil Department Store at 618 K Street. Gattmann also served as a director of the Capital National Bank until his retirement in 1922. (Courtesy McCurry Company Collection.)

William Low and his family built the house at 4433 T Street in 1928. Although William died in 1948, his wife, Christina, continued to live in the house until 1952. Low was in the hardware business with his partner, George H. Murray. The company was in several locations up and down J Street during the more than 20 years they were in business. (Courtesy *Suttertown News* Collection.)

Gilbert and Annie Beere built this house at 4733 T Street in 1923. Although they owned it for over 40 years, they never lived in the house, instead choosing to rent it out to salesmen, managers, clerks, and insurance agents. Gilbert was a salesman for Libby McNeil Libby cannery and other businesses. Annie operated a "grocerteria," a small market, in Sacramento. (Courtesy Ernest Myers Collection.)

George Friend and his sister Carol pose in front of their house at 1872 Fifty-third Street in 1950. The family built the house in 1943 at a cost of $3,000. Known today as "The Miracle on Fifty-third Street," the neighborhood around the Friend home has been lavishly decorated for the Christmas season since the mid-1990s. George dresses as Santa Claus and plays guitar and the saw. (Courtesy George Friend Collection.)

In 1939, on the outskirts of Elmhurst at about Fifty-ninth and S Streets, farmland still occupied the lots. This view is looking west at the home and farm of Emilio Puccinelli. He and his wife, Ida, and members of their large extended family worked the farm. The buildings were removed to allow for the construction of Highway 50. (Courtesy Eugene Hepting Collection.)

At the entrance to Elmhurst in 1933, Stockton Boulevard is still the major thoroughfare it was when called Upper Stockton Road. The trees along T Street, planted in the 1910s, are beginning to form the canopy that the street is famous for today. This view is looking southeast at the intersection. The signs on the gore point are advertising the Capital Lumber Company and the Associated Oil Company nearby. (Courtesy Bob McCabe Collection.)

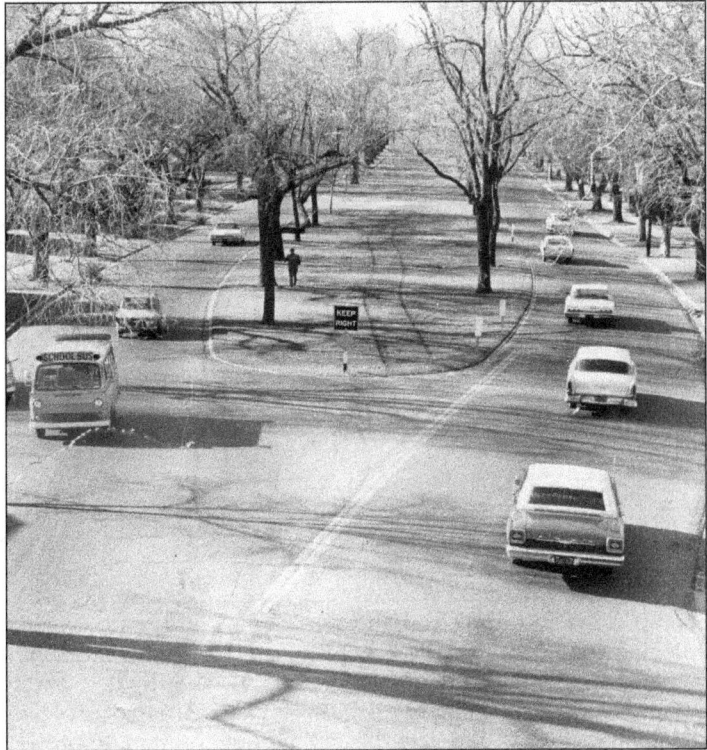

Bared for winter, this January 1968 image of T Street's trees in Elmhurst let the viewer see the broad expanse of the parkway. Suitably named Sunset Park on the west and Sierra View Park on the east, the two parkways are what give Elmhurst its distinction. The trees along T Street between Thirty-ninth and Fifty-third Streets are probably among the most photographed in Sacramento. (Courtesy *Sacramento Bee* Collection.)

In the spring of 1975, city maintenance workers sprayed insecticide on the trees on T Street for Dutch elm disease. Sacramento, known as the "City of Trees," fought valiantly to rid them of the disease. By 2003, the Sacramento Tree Foundation and its corps of volunteers planted thousands of new elm trees that arborists hope resist the disease. (Courtesy *Sacramento Bee* Collection.)

As the leaves are falling from the elms along T and Forty-seventh Streets, a bicyclist can be seen enjoying the ride under the canopy in this November 1983 view. Members of the community consider the Elmhurst neighborhood among the shadiest parts of Sacramento. The National Aeronautics and Space Administration conducted a flyover of Sacramento in 2000 and estimated the number of trees covering the city to be six million. (Courtesy *Sacramento Bee* Collection.)

The tree canopy along T Street can lower the summertime temperatures by 10 degrees. In addition to reducing the temperatures, the trees absorb the carbon dioxide and convert it to oxygen, creating cleaner air in the area. Homeowners, bicyclists, and other visitors benefit from these cooler climes. In this view from May 1981, an unidentified couple enjoys the quiet of the Elmhurst neighborhood. (Courtesy *Sacramento Bee* Collection.)

Sacramento built Elmhurst School in 1921 and renamed it Coloma the next year. The 1921 class poses here for their picture. Sixth from the left on the top row is Carlo Dallosta and to the left of the teacher, Mrs. Stanley, is Marjorie Cutler. The school became the Coloma Community Center in 1981, serving as host to neighborhood meetings, adult education classes, a community radio station, and youth programs. (Courtesy Marjorie Cutler Little Collection.)

In May 1922, the Sacramento Chamber of Commerce sponsored a citywide event called Days of '49 to celebrate the 1849 Gold Rush. Both teachers and students participated in donning period costumes. Coloma School principal, Mrs. Lagomarsino, is fourth from the left. First-grade students Virginia Howell (left) and Marjorie Cutler (right) are in the front row. (Courtesy Marjorie Cutler Little Collection.)

The Coloma School eighth-grade graduating class in 1938 had 15 students. The teacher, Miss Taylor, is on the far right. Carlo Dallosta, seated third from the right, was the best friend of the Peretti brothers, Henry and Albert, seated at far left and far right respectively. Frances Merlino, the second girl from the left, was a member of the family famous for bringing Merlino's Orange Freeze to Sacramento. (Courtesy Dolores Dallosta Collection.)

This view of the first-grade classroom at Coloma School in 1950–1951 shows the teacher, Mrs. Hill, standing in the background. All the students are smiling for the camera. George Friend shares a desk at right front center. Note that all the students sat two to a desk for their picture. (Courtesy George Friend Collection.)

The Coloma School, at 4623 T Street, sponsored a pet show parade in 1953. Principal Orrin Henderson, in his first year in that position, is on the left wearing the coat and tie. He watches as John Friend pulls his cousin George Friend in the "Black Panther Cage." The boys were in the third grade. The annual event brought family and friends to the school yard. (Courtesy George Friend Collection.)

Sacramento City Unified School District schools formerly graduated classes in January and June. This sixth-grade class from Coloma School poses for their class picture in January 1951. School photographer Michael Benning, whose studio was in North Sacramento, had the contract with the school district to photograph school classes in the area. (Courtesy Michael Benning Collection.)

In 1978, the Coloma School closed after 57 years of operation. It was slated for destruction, but instead the Sacramento City Council rescued the building by purchasing the property from the school district and then turning it into the present-day Coloma Community Center. They dedicated the center in 1981. Administered today by the parks and recreation department, the community center is a beehive of activities. (Courtesy City of Sacramento Collection.)

Two

TAHOE PARK
BY REBECCA CARRUTHERS
AND CARSON HENDRICKS

Before the Tahoe Park neighborhood developed, the land was agricultural and near the California State Fair grounds on Stockton Boulevard. The City of Sacramento purchased 19 acres for the Tahoe Park recreation facility in 1946, naming it after the adjacent school that opened in 1931. During and after World War II, returning veterans to Sacramento found the new homes in the Tahoe Park tracts affordable. Most of the single-family homes were two-bedroom, one-bath, and one-car garage structures on fairly large lots. Homes in the area sold for $7,000 in 1947. Because major transportation routes were available nearby, the Tahoe Park neighborhood was even more desirable. In this photograph, Charles Haslam poses outside his new house at 2624 Fifty-third Street in August 1942. Charles and his wife, Lucille, had just moved into the Tahoe Park neighborhood. During World War II, Charles worked for the Sacramento Air Depot. The Haslams would live there until 1952, when Rex A. Wertz and his wife, Myra, moved in. Rex worked for the California State Department of Justice. (Courtesy Cindy Baker Collection.)

In 1912, a crew of laborers building the home at 2429 Upper Stockton Road, as it was known before it became Stockton Boulevard, pause to have their photograph taken. Joseph Tuchfarber, a local plasterer by trade, completed building his home in 1915. Joseph and his wife, Mary Frances, continued to live in the house until Joseph's death in 1927. (Courtesy Packard de Flores Collection.)

After the death of Joseph Tuchfarber, widow Mary Frances married Packard de Flores in 1930. They continued to live in the house until her death. Packard remarried his longtime nurse, Alice, and lived in the house until his death in 1972. According to the city directories, Packard was a businessman, farmer, and vintner. This view of the house is from around 1920, before Stockton Boulevard was paved. (Courtesy Packard de Flores Collection.)

Charles R. Wise and his wife, Leslie, took out a permit to build this house at 6255 Fourteenth Avenue in 1921. Wise was a clerk for the Pioneer Fruit Company and would take four years to build the house at a cost of $4,000. In 1930, John Sarzotti and his wife, Margaret, moved into the house and added a summer kitchen in the basement. (Courtesy Bob McCabe Collection.)

The eastern city limits of Sacramento were primarily farmland at Sixty-fifth Street and Fifth Avenue. This view, taken on November 4, 1939, is looking west toward Sacramento. Within 10 years, many returning World War II veterans and their families would build homes on this farmland in the new Tahoe Park subdivision. Houses and lots cost $7,000. (Courtesy Eugene Hepting Collection.)

....*TECHNICALLY*

Speaking . . . .

We introduce you here to our staff of technicians. You never hear these fellows on the KROY airwaves, yet their work is vitally essential to bringing programs into your home. Working quietly behind the scenes, each is licensed by the Government to perform his particular duties on the KROY technical staff.

HOWARD MARTINEAU

MARC JOHNSEN

JOHN O'CONNOR

WINSTON BULL

KROY signed on the air in 1937. The call letters were chosen to honor station owner Royal Miller. KROY entertained Sacramentans for 40 years. KROY's heyday was 1968 through 1973, when it was known as "the 1240 Rock." KROY had loyal listeners who enjoyed the high visibility of the disc jockeys attending many community events. This image is taken from a 1948 KROY promotional brochure. (Courtesy Bill Stritzel Collection.)

KROY's transmitter and tower were located on a street appropriately named KROY Way. From late 1950s to mid-1960s, the radio station was located at 1010 Eleventh Street in downtown Sacramento. In 1966, it moved to 977 Arden Way, where listeners could watch their favorite disc jockeys through a curbside window. KROY endeared itself to listeners by showing up at events with an antique fire truck painted with the station's trademark shade of purple. (Courtesy Eugene Hepting Collection.)

Houses and lots in the Tahoe Park area called the Sierra View Terrace Tract cost $4,000 in 1939. There were 125 lots in the tract with 27 homes under construction. Len Kidder poses next to the "sold" sign, and behind him is the William and Clara Sherman home at 3351 Fifty-sixth Street. William was a brakeman for the Southern Pacific Railroad. (Courtesy Eugene Hepting Collection.)

The construction site at Fifty-fifth Street and Eighth Avenue in December 1939 shows the houses underway. Pacific Gas & Electric Company (PG&E) workers are seen erecting the power poles for the neighborhood. The photographer, Eugene Hepting, identified Jimmy Callaway at left center, observing two workers stringing cables to one of the poles. (Courtesy Eugene Hepting Collection.)

Robert and Beverly Sickels, with their son Robert Jr. and daughter Suzanne, stand proudly in front of their home at 3360 Sixty-second Street in May 1951. The family was dressed up for Suzanne Sickels's first communion at All Hallows Church. The Sickels moved into their new home on October 31, 1947. The backyard was across from Tahoe Park where the Sickels' children enjoyed many playful days. (Courtesy Robert Sickels Family Collection.)

Suzanne Sickels makes a purchase of ice cream from the neighborhood ice cream man in the summer of 1951. Suzanne, the oldest of four children in the Sickels family, grew up on Sixty-second Street. Buying ice cream was a common occurrence throughout the hot Sacramento summers. Children looked forward to flagging down the cheerful-sounding ice cream truck and enjoying a nice, cold treat. (Courtesy Robert Sickels Family Collection.)

The Condos daughters, Carrie and Susan, laugh with their friends Maria Gonzales (left) and John and Jim Procida in the front yard of their house on 5836 Thirteenth Avenue in 1963. The Condos family lived in that house from 1958 until 1969. The Condos children attended All Hallows Parish School. Procida was a well-known name in Sacramento due to their florist and landscaping businesses. (Courtesy Condos Family Collection.)

The Tallac Village Square Shops sign on Fourteenth Avenue flashed from top to bottom, delighting neighborhood children. Thomas P. Raley, who founded the grocery chain in 1935, dominated the grocery business in Sacramento after World War II. Notice the Blue Chip Stamps sign on the left. Stores gave out the stamps, and customers could redeem books of stamps for appliances such as toasters. (Courtesy *Sacramento Bee* Collection.)

Seen from the other direction, Tallac Village Square Shops in the early 1950s offered convenient shopping for the families living in Tahoe Park. Similar in design to the new Town and Country Shopping Center, with wooden shake roofs, shrubs, and ivy covering the walls, Tallac Village boasted a grocery, hardware, and variety stores. Through the years, popular gathering places were Tallac Lounge and Tallac Village Barbershop. (Courtesy *Sacramento Bee* Collection.)

By 1950, the intersection of Stockton Boulevard and Broadway were major thoroughfares with traffic congestion as shown here. The Sacramento Planning Commission and the Sacramento City Council developed a community master plan for the site known as the East Broadway Area. To relieve the congestion around the county hospital and state fairgrounds, the master plan suggested moving the fairgrounds to a larger facility. (Courtesy California Department of Transportation, © 1950.)

The Fireman's Relief and Protective Association, an organization of firemen, financed the construction of two firehouses in 1933, including Engine Company No. 9 at Sixth Avenue and Stockton Boulevard, seen here. The association built the firehouses and then leased them back to the city with an option to purchase, thus saving the city's funds during the financially strapped Depression years. (Courtesy City of Sacramento Collection.)

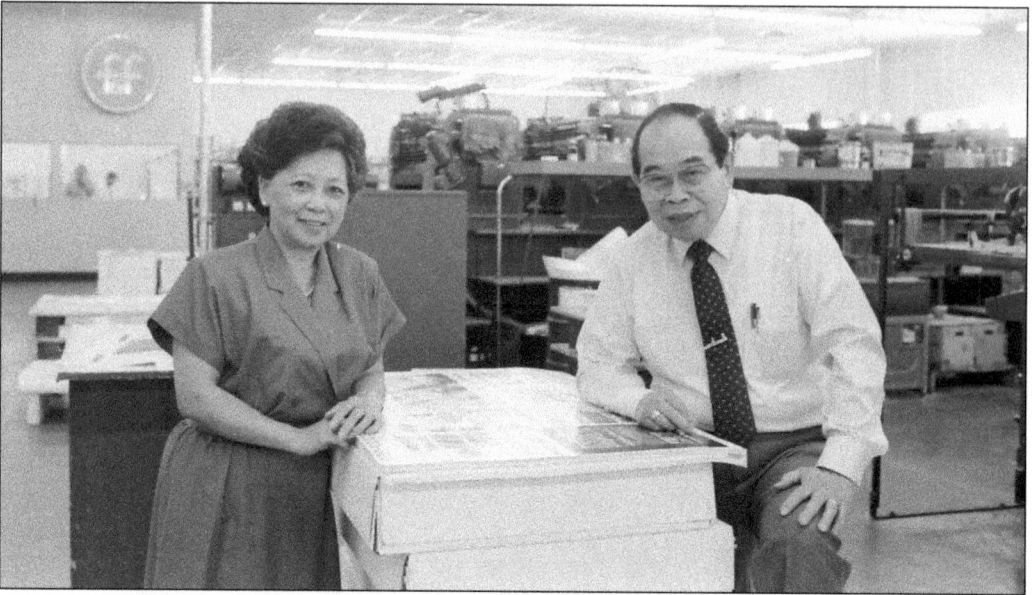

Fong and Fong Printers, started by Mae and Paul Fong at a Sixteenth and V Streets location in 1960, moved to a 31,000-square-foot plant near Sixty-fifth Street and Highway 50 in 1980, part of a 5-acre industrial park. Their business was the first Asian American printing company in Sacramento and one of the first in Northern California. Paul passed away in 2006. (Courtesy *Sacramento Bee* Collection.)

William Ridgeway Family Relations Courthouse on Power Inn Road is called a "family relations" courthouse because it includes all family-law courtrooms in addition to support services related to family and juvenile cases. Two hundred county employees work in the 165,000-square-foot building that opened at the end of 1999. The modern courthouse has more windows and people-friendly gathering areas than previous county courthouses. (Courtesy *Sacramento Bee* Collection.)

In 1953, the Bethany Assembly of God Church on the corner of Sixty-fifth Street and Fourteenth Avenue held Sunday services in the Tahoe Park neighborhood. John H. Hamilton served as pastor until 1960. Situated across the street from Hiram Johnson High School, the building is now home to St. Philip the Apostle Byzantine Catholic Church, a Greek Orthodox Church. (Courtesy Frank Christy Collection.)

On November 29, 1942, residents of Tahoe Park and Colonial Heights dedicated their own Catholic church at 5501 Fourteenth Avenue. The interior seated 400 persons. The residing pastor was Rev. Michael McGoldrick. In 1960, Bishop Joseph McGucken dedicated the new All Hallows Church. In 1977, parishioners of St. Peter's Church voted to purchase the old parish building and move it to their property on McMahon Drive. (Courtesy Michael Benning Collection.)

Tahoe School opened in 1931 at 5932 Fifth Avenue as a kindergarten through sixth-grade elementary school. It served the residents in the Tahoe Park neighborhood until the population began increasing with the influx of families after World War II. In January 1948, the campus expanded to meet the needs of the new students with the addition of these new buildings. (Courtesy *Sacramento Bee* Collection.)

Seen in 1949 after the expansion of the campus from its original four rooms, Tahoe School changed its address to 5924 Broadway after Fifth Avenue became Broadway in 1938. It continues to be a vital part of the community today but again at a new address, 3110 Sixtieth Street, after the school reconfigured its administration building. (Courtesy *Sacramento Bee* Collection.)

All Hallows Parish School opened in 1948 to meet the needs of new families settling in the neighborhood after World War II. The school was staffed by the Sisters of Charity of the Blessed Virgin Mary. Msgr. Patrick Corkell was instrumental in the building of the parish hall and gymnasium constructed in 1977. In 2005, the Sisters Servants of the Blessed Sacrament assumed the administration of the school. (Courtesy Robert Sickels Family Collection.)

On January 24, 1992, a truckload of snow from Crystal Ice was delivered to the Marian Anderson Elementary School at 2850 Forty-ninth Street as students began their Mitten Parade around the schoolyard. The school was celebrating Mitten Week, based on a Ukrainian folktale the children were studying. The event offered many their first experience of playing in snow. (Courtesy *Sacramento Bee* Collection.)

Hiram Johnson High School had a very active social scene. The school, on September 24, 1960, held the sophomore reception to welcome incoming sophomores. There was also an election for class officers. The theme for the event, which included music and dancing, was beatniks. Seen here preparing for the reception are Nancy O'Donnell (front), Janet Lockhard (left), and Clifford Bennet. (Courtesy *Sacramento Bee* Collection.)

The senior prom for Hiram Johnson High School was held at Arden Hills Swimming and Tennis Club on June 16, 1960. Seen here walking on the grounds are, from left to right, Lee DeLange, Sandi Johnson, Kathy Witsell, and Jerry Curtis. (Courtesy *Sacramento Bee* Collection.)

Hiram Johnson High School provided Home Economics classes for the female students. Classes taught young women how to sew, cook, and be a successful homemaker. In April 1962, teacher Virginia Eoff (left) looks on as a student gives a sewing demonstration. (Courtesy *Sacramento Bee* Collection.)

A fire broke out near the boy's locker room at the Hiram Johnson High School gymnasium in November 1972. The school had recently been the target of vandals. The room where the fire started was broken into and the lock damaged. Fire damage was minor, with the gymnasium bearing the brunt of it. About 40 students were evacuated from the gym, but no one was hurt. (Courtesy *Sacramento Bee* Collection.)

The lush green of Tahoe Park, located at Eighth Avenue and Fifty-ninth Streets, is an oasis in the middle of the residential area named after the park. The City of Sacramento purchased the park's 19 acres of land in 1946 at a cost of $28,045. Visitors to the park enjoy picnic areas, playgrounds, ball fields, volleyball and basketball courts, a swimming pool, a horseshoe pit, and a community facility. (Courtesy Rebecca Carruthers.)

City of Sacramento's Tahoe Park provides the neighborhood children with many activities. A ventriloquist in the community facility entertains his audience with a dummy sidekick. This photograph was taken at the local talent show on Easter Day in 1957. (Courtesy City of Sacramento Collection.)

Baseball was a popular activity at Tahoe Park when it first opened in 1946. Among the earliest amenities built was the baseball field. This photograph from 1960 shows a game in progress at the park. The Giants, sponsored by Crystal Dairy, plays an unidentified team; David Gray is the catcher. Visible in the background is the expanded Tahoe School. (Courtesy Judith Gray Allen Collection.)

The Indians Little League team poses for this photograph at Tahoe Park in 1961. The coaches are Robert Sickels, at left in the third row, and Tony Ivanovich, at right in the third row; Robert Sickels Jr. is standing at the far right in the second row. Today Tahoe Park ball fields are used primarily for youth softball leagues. (Courtesy Robert Sickels Family Collection.)

This June 1974 photograph shows the Greenfair Towers II just before its dedication. The 194 units in the building are one-bedroom apartments containing 628 square feet, including a 100-hundred-square-foot balcony. Greenfair Towers II was completed in rough form in just 18 days using the FCE-Dillon module system developed by the U.S. Department of Housing and Urban Development's Operation Breakthrough program. Greenfair Towers I and Greenfair Towers II were established exclusively for those of retirement age who qualify under specified income requirements or anyone having a certified physical handicap. Conducting the dedication was the Retirement Housing Foundation of Long Beach, part of the Council of Health and Welfare Agencies of the United Church of Christ. The building was designed by Ogren, Juarez, and Givas and built by Campbell Construction Company, both of Sacramento. The Greenfair Towers are on Broadway near Stockton Boulevard. (Courtesy *Sacramento Bee* Collection.)

Three

THE COLONIALS
BY LISA C. PRINCE

Caught on camera are three young boys out for a springtime ride beneath the palm-treed canopy along San Francisco Boulevard, once the entryway to an estate of vast vineyards. When built in 1910, developers of the Colonial Heights subdivision constructed the wide thoroughfare into three separate lanes. By the time this photograph was taken in 1964, the area had developed into affordable suburban neighborhoods that encompassed the adjacent subdivided areas known as Colonial Acres, Colonial Village, and Colonial Manor, long ago known as The Heights. In 1910, George Peltier, a Sacramento banker and developer who later built the Alhambra Theater, first subdivided the area and promoted its development. Peltier was earlier involved in the building of the Central California Traction Company, a passenger and freight service that provided residents with transportation to and from Sacramento. The area grew steadily for several years and then tapered off during the years before World War II. In 1948, fearing an increase in taxes, many residents in The Heights opposed annexation, but it was voted in and the area was added to the fast-growing city of Sacramento. (Courtesy *Sacramento Bee* Collection.)

Announced in the May 7, 1910, *Sacramento Bee* was the grand opening of Colonial Heights, "Sacramento's ideal subdivision." Highlighted were enticing selling points such as free life insurance, pure water, large lots, and 5¢ rapid-transit fares. The advertisement claims that Colonial Heights was the first subdivision opened in any city with the unique advantage of a magnificent interurban electric line running to it. (Courtesy *Sacramento Bee* Collection.)

Looking south from the city limits is this 1913 long shot of Stockton Boulevard south of Fourteenth Avenue. The tracks of the Central California Traction Company are to the left of the lightly traveled, unpaved boulevard where a couple of automobiles share the wide road with a lone pedestrian. Several new homes can be seen alongside the endless stretch of power lines. (Courtesy California Department of Transportation, © 1913.)

The Roemer Castle, off Stockton Boulevard, was built around the turn of the 20th century in the area subdivided into Colonial Heights. In 1881, Peter Roemer immigrated to the United States from Germany and to California two years later. His 240-acre vineyard was considered one of the finest in Northern California. Later Franz Dicks lived in the home and taught private violin lessons there. (Courtesy Franz Dicks Collection.)

47

Seated on the porch of their farmhouse, on what would later be subdivided into Colonial Heights, are Philip and Margeretta Greule with their twin daughters, Katherine and Mary, around 1911. Philip came to Sacramento from San Francisco after the devastating 1906 earthquake, where he met and married Margeretta in 1907. The farmhouse was situated on land that spans today's Fifty-eighth and Sixtieth Streets, along Twenty-first Avenue. (Courtesy Matilda Greule Collection.)

Price List of Unsold Lots in COLONIAL ACRES — J. C. CARLY CO.

623 J St. Phone Main 351

LOT	IMPROVEMENT	PRICE	LOT	IMPROVEMENT	PRICE	LOT	IMPROVEMENT	PRICE
2	Windmill, Wine Grapes, few Cherries	$1050.00	49	Table Grapes	1250.00	120	Vacant	750.00
3	Wine Grapes, Barn	1050.00	50	Table Grapes	1200.00	121	Vacant	750.00
4	Wine Grapes	850.60	51	Table Grapes	1300.00	122	Vacant	750.00
5	Wine Grapes	850.00	52	Peaches, Cherries	1460.00	123	Vacant	850.00
6	Wine Grapes	850.00	53	Peaches	2000.00	124	Vacant	850.00
7	Wine Grapes	850.00	56	Table Grapes, Apples, Figs	1800.00	125	Vacant	750.00
8	Wine Grapes	850.00	57	Vacant	1600.00	126	Vacant	750.00
9	Wine Grapes	850.00	58	Vacant	1300.00	127	Vacant	750.06
10	Vacant	900.00	59	Vacant	1100.00	140	Vacant	700.00
11	Vacant	900.00	60	Table Grapes	1200.00	141	Vacant	750.00
12	Wine Grapes	900.00	61	Table Grapes	1300.00	142	Vacant	750.00
13	Vacant	900.00	62	Table Grapes	1360.00	143	Vacant	850.00
18	Table Grapes	1700.00	63	Table Grapes	1300.00	144	Vacant	850.00
19	Vacant	1600.00	64	Table Grapes	1200.00	145	Vacant	750.00
20	Vacant	1500.00	65	Table Grapes	1200.00	146	Vacant	750.00
21	Table Grapes, Almonds	1200.00	66	Table Grapes	1200.00	147	Vacant	750.00
23	Almonds, Cherries, Berries	1200.00	67	Table Grapes	1300.00	148	Vacant	750.00
24	Grapes	1100.00	72	Berries, Grapes	1200.00	149	Vacant	750.00
25	Table Grapes, Cherries	1000.00	73	Garden, Strawberries	1200.00	150	Vacant	750.00
26	Wine Grapes, Cherries	950.00	80	Peaches, Berries	950.00	151	Vacant	750.00
27	Wine Grapes, Cherries	900.00	81	½ Grapes, Raspberries, 2 Mills	1150.00	154	Orchard, Vineyard	750.00
28	Wine Grapes, Cherries	900.00	86	Vacant	950.00	155	Vacant	650.00
29	Wine Grapes, Pears	1000.00	87	Vacant	900.00	156	Vacant	650.00
30	Wine Grapes	950.00	89	Vacant	850.00	157	Vacant	650.00
31	Wine Grapes	850.00	99	Vacant	550.00	158	Vacant	650.00
32	Wine Grapes	850.00	101	Vacant	750.00	159	Vacant	650.00
33	Wine Grapes	850.00	102	Vacant	850.00	160	Vacant	650.00
34	Wine Grapes	850.00	103	Vacant	850.00	161	Vacant	750.00
35	Wine Grapes	850.00	104	Vacant	850.00	162	Vacant	750.00
36	Wine Grapes, Pears	850.00	105	Vacant	9?0.00	163	Vacant	650.00
37	Wine Grapes, Pears	900.00	106	Vacant	950.00	165	Vacant	650.00
38	Wine Grapes, Pears	1100.00	107	Vacant	900.00	172	Vacant	850.00
39	Peaches, Plums	1250.00	108	Vacant	900.00	173	Vacant	850.00
40	Vacant	1050.00	109	Vacant	900.00	174	Vacant	1050.00
41	Vacant	1050.00	110	Vacant	900.00	175	Vacant	1050.00
42	Vacant	1050.00	111	Vacant	900.00	176	Vacant	1150.00
43	Part Grapes	1050.00	112	Vacant	900.00	177	Vacant	1250.00
44	Part Grapes	1100.00	113	Vacant	900.00	178	Vacant	1250.00
45	Part Grapes	1100.00	114	Vacant	1050.00	181	Vacant	1350.00
46	Part Grapes	1100.00	115	Vacant	850.00	182	Vacant	1250.00
47	Part Grapes	1250.00	116	Vacant	750.00	183	Vacant	1250.00
48	Part Table Grapes	1300.00	117	Vacant	750.00	184	Vacant	1250.00
			118	Vacant	750.00	185	Vacant	1250.00
			119	Vacant	750.00	187	Vacant	1300.00

TERMS: 15 per cent cash; $10 per month per acre; 5 per cent discount for all cash.

This is a c. 1915 price list of unsold lots in the new Colonial Acres subdivision offered by the J. C. Carley Company of Sacramento, which had taken over operations from George Peltier. Evident are the many vacant lots as well as those improved with the various crops grown in the area's rich soils: wine grapes, cherries, almonds, berries, pears, peaches, plums, strawberries, raspberries, apples, and figs. (Courtesy Matilda Greule Collection.)

A large undeveloped parcel owned by the Wright Holding Company, between Fruitridge Road and the Central California Traction Company line on Twenty-first Avenue, is the focal point in this c. 1948 photograph. The area south of Fruitridge Road shows new development on large lots with vacant tracts to the right. The California State Fair grounds are surrounded by dense and booming growth. (Courtesy Frank Christy Collection.)

Surrounded by family and friends, Walter C. Stratton, chairman of the Fruitridge-Colonial Heights annexation committee, sits on his front porch at 4924 Fourteenth Avenue in the summer of 1948. Walter moved to California from Michigan in 1945. Standing to Walter's right are his daughter "Punky," his wife, Fern, and eldest daughter, Sandy. Joining them are neighbors smiling for the camera. (Courtesy Walter C. Stratton Collection.)

This is an advertisement from the February 19, 1948, issue of the *Chronicle*, an independent, progressive newspaper published in south Sacramento. Citizens were beseeched to vote for the annexation of Fruitridge-Colonial Heights to the City of Sacramento on March 2, 1948. Joining the city, proponents claimed, would save residents $1.63 per $100 in taxes whether or not they had children in school. It would also relieve overcrowding at the Fruitridge School by allowing the Sacramento City Unified School Board to purchase a plot of land in the district for the construction of a new school. Moreover, police and fire protection would be extended to the district. Residents voted 638 to 584 in favor of annexation to Sacramento. It was approved by the city council on March 12 and 1,277 acres and approximately 5,000 residents were added to the growing city. (Courtesy Walter C. Stratton Collection.)

On May 13, 1964, cars were trapped and lawns swamped in deep water in this Colonial Heights neighborhood. Residents were immobilized by the floodwaters of Morrison Creek. City engineers advised passage of drainage measures to insure improved drainage in the city's populated areas to avoid scenes such as these in the future. (Courtesy *Sacramento Bee* Collection.)

The tremendous growth of the area is evident in this 1953 aerial photograph that shows the intersection of Stockton Boulevard and Fruitridge Road in the foreground. Fifty-eighth Street bisects the land to the right, and the state fairgrounds can be seen in the upper left corner. The Fruitridge Drive-in to the left opened in the summer of 1950. (Courtesy California Department of Transportation, © 1953.)

51

Proud proprietors stand before a well-stocked case of fresh produce in this interior shot of Loverde's Market on Fruitridge Road in 1947. The market opened in 1946 and, in addition to fruits and vegetables, sold fresh meats as well as other grocery items. Loverde's Market operated until the 1963 death of partner Victor J. Cima, pictured on the right. (Courtesy Alice Ciani Collection.)

Loverde's Variety at 6804 Fruitridge Road was operated by William and Lillian Loverde, longtime residents of the area. One can see items of clothing, notions, and assorted household items in the window displays of this c. 1950 photograph. Loverde's Hardware and Variety at 6800 Fruitridge operated at this location until 1968. (Courtesy Harry Sweet Collection.)

After selling the produce grown on their family farm in Placer County out of a used truck, and operating a small store in Penryn, the Wong family built their first supermarket in Sacramento on Fruitridge Road in 1955. The family business grew tremendously and in 1992 merged with a former competitor, Raley's. Stores now reach as far north as Yuba City and east to Cameron Park. (Courtesy Raley's.)

In this 1986 photograph inside the Bel Air on Fruitridge Road, Bill Wong holds a portrait of his father, Gim Wong, the family patriarch who immigrated to California from China in 1922. By the 1930s, the Wong family was selling the fruits and vegetables grown at their farm in Penryn. From its humble beginnings, the goal of the Wong's fast-growing supermarket business was to offer the best possible products and customer service. (Courtesy *Sacramento Bee* Collection.)

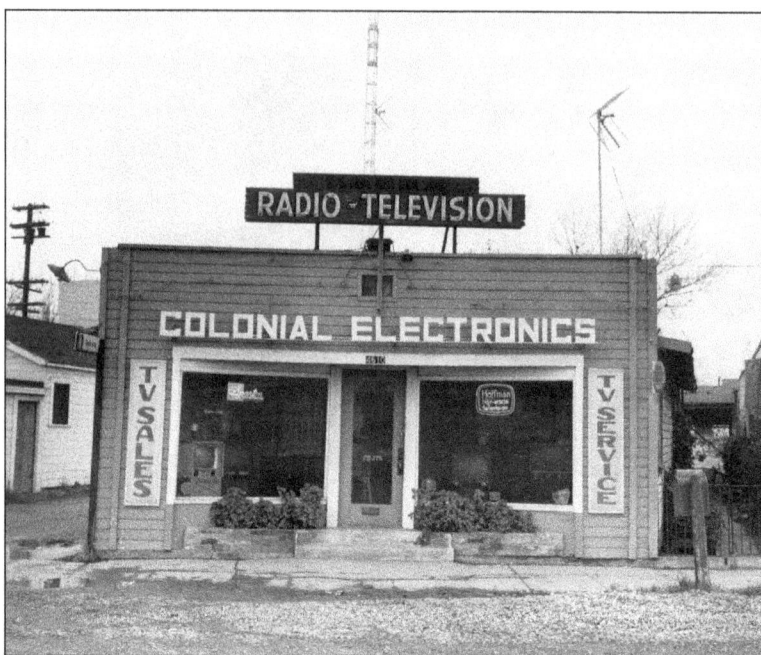

This is a 1950s photograph of Colonial Electronics at 4610 Stockton Boulevard where owner Paul J. Beihler offered radio and television sales and service. Television was a relatively new medium in the 1950s, as is demonstrated by the various large and bulky sets displayed in the window. (Courtesy Harry Sweet Collection.)

Parked in front of Fruitridge Radio and Television, located at the Fruitridge Shopping Center on Stockton Boulevard, are two company vehicles—Nos. 7 and 8—advertising the store's products and services. This 1950s-era photograph is representative of the variety of small shops and businesses that grew out of the multiplying needs and desires of the area's booming population. (Courtesy Harry Sweet Collection.)

This is a c. 1947 menu from Frasinetti's Fine Foods, located at the intersection of Stockton and San Francisco Boulevards. The menu boasts of such delectable fares as Veal Scallopini a la Marsala for $1.75 and Chicken a la Frasinetti for $2.25. The Frasinettis were pioneers in the region's wine industry and continue to operate their restaurant at the site of their winery in Florin, established in 1897. (Courtesy Sacramento Public Library, Sacramento Room.)

Seen here is the 1950s catering wagon of George E. Johnson's Del Prado Restaurant, the self-proclaimed "home of mahogany-broiled steaks," at Fruitridge Road and Stockton Boulevard. The restaurant specialized in continental cuisine, banquets and luncheons, and complete catering services. The popular eatery featured gardens, a patio, and a sunken piano room, "Sacramento's most colorful lounge." George's son Eppie followed in his father's footsteps with his own chain of restaurants that bore his name. (Courtesy Eppie G. Johnson Collection.)

The magnificent mausoleum of St. Mary's is pictured here in 1942. The 60-acre cemetery and mausoleum opened in 1929 at Twenty-first Avenue and Sixty-fifth Street and contains more than 35,000 interments. Many area notables rest here: legendary baseball players, state and federal politicians and practitioners of law, several thousand veterans, and the famous world boxing champion, Max Baer, and his wife, Mary. (Courtesy Ralph Shaw Collection.)

Facing Twenty-first Avenue, St. Mary's Cemetery is the large plot seen in the middle of this 1979 aerial photograph. To the right is Sacramento County's graveyard for indigents, known as Potter's Field from the 1920s to the 1940s. In 1975, the Catholic Diocese agreed to acquire the land and maintain it in exchange for land to expand St. Mary's. A 2-acre portion is reserved for deceased veterans. (Courtesy *Sacramento Bee* Collection.)

Pictured is Mac Aguilar Jr. tending his father's grave at St. Mary's Cemetery around 1995. Joining him are sons Andrew and Danny, who carefully sweep their grandfather's grave-site marker while their father tidies up the edges. They also placed the bouquet of fresh flowers seen in the foreground. (Courtesy *Catholic Herald* Collection.)

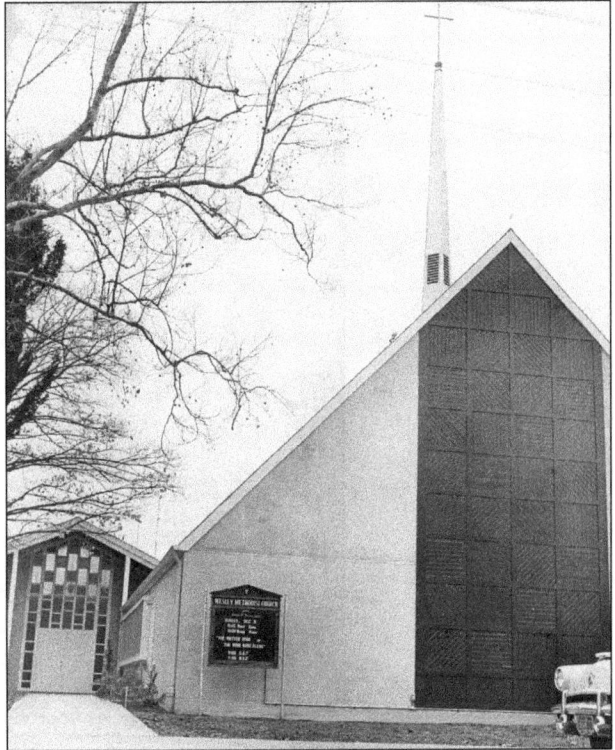

The Wesley Methodist Church, located at 5010 Fifteenth Avenue, was founded at this site in 1914. In that year's city directory, the church was listed at Vina Vista near Upper Stockton Road, which became Fifteenth Avenue after city growth required street name changes in 1916. The new church structure, built in the late 1950s, is shown in this photograph. (Courtesy Frank Christy Collection.)

A half-dozen determined crossing guards march toward their safety program duties at Mark Twain Elementary School at 4914 Fifty-eighth Street in this 1965 photograph. The school was one of several built in the early 1950s due to phenomenal growth of the city and recently annexed areas. (Courtesy *Sacramento Bee* Collection.)

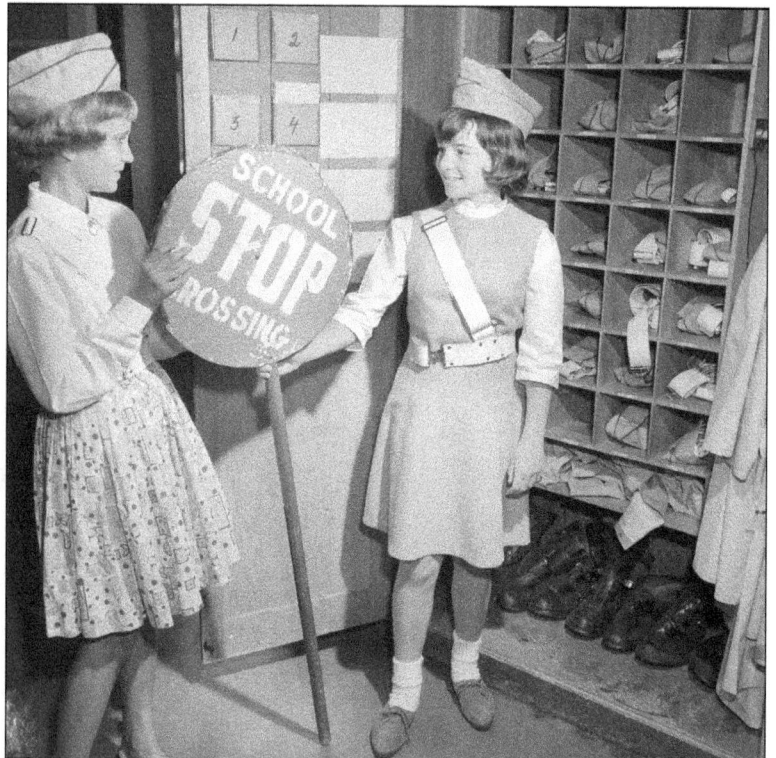

Two Mark Twain Elementary students, holding a well-used school-crossing stop sign and outfitted in the school's safety program's caps and belts, smile for the camera as they prepare for their crossing guard duties. (Courtesy *Sacramento Bee* Collection.)

Four-year-old preschooler Andrea Wynne comes eye to eye with this baby lamb during the annual Farm Day, sponsored by the Sacramento City Unified School District and the Sacramento County Farm Bureau on November 30, 1990. Students at Earl Warren Elementary School at Lowell Street and Fruitridge Road were given a hands-on experience with a variety of animals such as horses, rabbits, pigs, sheep, cattle, pygmy goats, chickens, geese, and more. (Courtesy *Sacramento Bee* Collection.)

Miwok dancers Damian Olvera (facing camera) and Donnie Villa participate in the Rabbit Dance with a smiling Miko Shimosaka and Christine Anderson during a Multicultural Fair at West Campus High School in April 1994. The three-day festival featured a variety of ethnic foods, art, a Native American jewelry exhibit, crafts demonstrations, and Hmong and Filipino dances. (Courtesy *Sacramento Bee* Collection.)

This is the interior of the Colonial Heights Library at the corner of Fifty-fourth Street and Seventeenth Avenue in 1951. The library was named for Mabel Gillis, the area's first librarian. In 1989, a new 12,000-square-foot building replaced the Mabel Gillis, Fruitridge, and Oak Park Libraries. The facility serves people in the surrounding 9-square-mile area. (Courtesy Sacramento Public Library, Sacramento Room.)

Celebrating the five-year anniversary of the Colonial Heights Library in 1994, the Folklor Mexicano De Sacramento performs a traditional Mexican folk dance in colorful regional dress. The group traced Mexico's history in narration and traditional dance and dress from various regions. Guests of honor were Sacramento mayor Joe Serna, council member Deborah Ortiz, board of supervisors member Illa Collin, and Sacramento Public Library administration. (Courtesy *Sacramento Bee* Collection.)

A happy group of Bluebirds pose in Matilda Greule's backyard at 5833 Twentieth Avenue in May 1958. Matilda's daughter Linda, standing at left, joined her friends for fun-filled activities and community projects. The Bluebird program, part of the Camp Fire Girls, was officially introduced for younger girls and offered exploration of ideas and creative play built around family and community life. (Courtesy Matilda Greule Collection.)

The Royals, a Southeastern Pony League baseball team, poses with the coaches in this 1964 photograph at Kirby Field. The baseball field was located at 6487 Fruitridge Road, next to St. Mary's Field No. 2 at 6485 Fruitridge Road where the Fruitridge Little League played. In 1966, Kirby Field was renamed James Rowell Babe Ruth League Baseball Park. (Courtesy McCurry Company Collection.)

In 1948, state and city fire authorities condemned as unsafe the Fairhaven Hospital and Home for unmarried mothers, built in 1913 and located at 4480 Sixty-third Street. The Reverend and Mrs. Manie Payne founded the Penial Mission in Sacramento in 1898 on Second and K Streets. By 1948, Fairhaven had given aid to nearly 6,000 "friendless girls." Public fund-raising efforts helped construct a new, modern facility in 1949. (Courtesy *Sacramento Bee* Collection.)

The new, modernized Fairhaven Home was reopened in the Colonial Acres neighborhood at 4360 Sixty-third Street in 1950. It was equipped with beds for 40 patients, both pre- and post-natal care, and a nursery capacity of 20. The equipment included a labor, delivery, and emergency surgery room, kitchen, laundry, and other units. Due to financial problems, Fairhaven closed in 1979. (Courtesy *Sacramento Bee* Collection.)

Four

BUSINESS AND INDUSTRY IN THE DISTRICT
BY PATRICIA J. JOHNSON

The Fruitridge Shopping Center in the southern Sacramento suburbs represented the wave of the future when it opened after World War II. The shopping center model developed differently from earlier business and industries in the region. As the city annexed territory to the east and south in 1911, enterprises located their ventures in the new area, which in turn provided services for the families moving into new subdivisions. Theaters opened, a bottling company relocated to the region, and restaurants, grocery stores, and other retailers provided conveniently located services to people in the new neighborhoods. Major manufacturing and military industries also established their operations in the district. Geographically, the area around the developing district encompassed more than 14 square miles. The abundant vacant land enticed lumberyards, box factories, soap makers, and the U.S. Army to locate here and would subsequently supply the livelihood for many of the nearby families. This 1950s view of the center shows a grocery store, a soda fountain with a lunch counter, and a hardware store. (Courtesy *Sacramento Bee* Collection.)

The Colonial Theater, an art deco–style, 500-seat movie house, opened as a premiere theater June 7, 1940, at 3522 Stockton Boulevard near Eighth Avenue. For more than 30 years, patrons from the neighborhood enjoyed first-run movies. Seen here in the final stages of construction, the theater's original owner, Charlie Joseph Holtz, also included a "crying room" where parents could sit with their infants during the movie. (Courtesy Eugene Hepting Collection.)

At a cost of more than $200,000 for renovations, the Colonial Theater reopened in 1996 after a four-year hiatus. Owner Jaime Santillan purchased the theater in 1978 and began showing Mexican-produced films. With a loan from the Sacramento Housing and Redevelopment Agency, Santillan was able to refurbish the 56-year-old theater. The building also hosted rock and rap concerts and boxing and wrestling matches. (Courtesy *Sacramento Bee* Collection.)

In 1962, Burich's Grill and Charcoal Broiler was a popular eatery at 4217 Stockton Boulevard. Run by James A. Burich and his son, they advertised that they were just "a few short blocks from the state fair." Originally the location was Frasinetti's Fine Food Restaurant, which operated as a restaurant and liquor store from 1940 until the Burichs took over in 1954. (Courtesy *Sacramento Bee* Collection.)

In its heyday during the 1950s, the Cardinal Grocery Stores had more than 16 outlets around Sacramento. A leading chain store, the markets became a division of Lucky Stores in 1960. In this 1940s view at 3750 Stockton Boulevard, taken during the holiday season, note the Christmas tree sticking out of the trunk of the parked 1947 Chevrolet. (Courtesy *Sacramento Bee* Collection.)

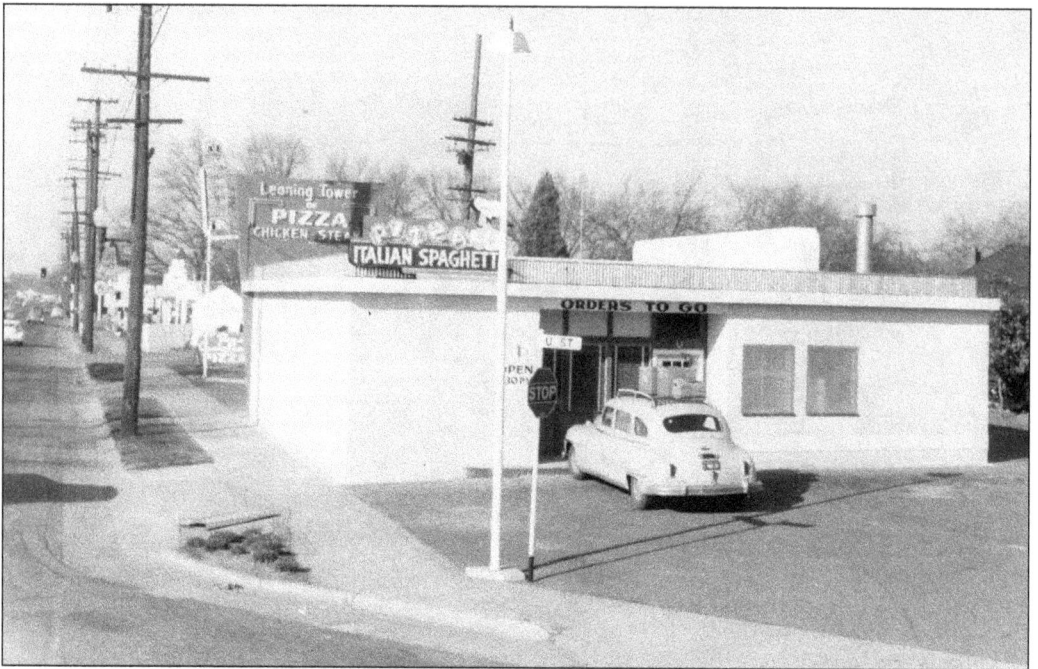

The Leaning Tower of Pizza attracted a lot of attention with its iconic play on words. The Italian restaurant, on the southeast corner 2033 Stockton Boulevard and U Streets, did a brisk business during the 1960s and 1970s. Today Stockton Burgers occupies the site and except for the missing leaning tower, the building remains the same. (Courtesy Harry Sweet Collection.)

Pacific Telephone and Telegraph Company opened the new South Dial Office at 2216 Stockton Boulevard in 1941. David W. Joslyn, who worked in the building, took this c. 1945 picture of his wife, Beverly Cotton Joslyn, standing outside the office. The company continued to operate at that location through the 1970s. (Courtesy Penny Joslyn Howorth Collection.)

Over the years, a number of businesses occupied this building at 3836 Stockton Boulevard. Charles and Ann Chamberlain opened Chamberlain's Electrical Appliances in 1947 and changed the name to Colonial Home Appliances in 1949. They continued in business until 1958, when a furniture business took over the site. (Courtesy Harry Sweet Collection.)

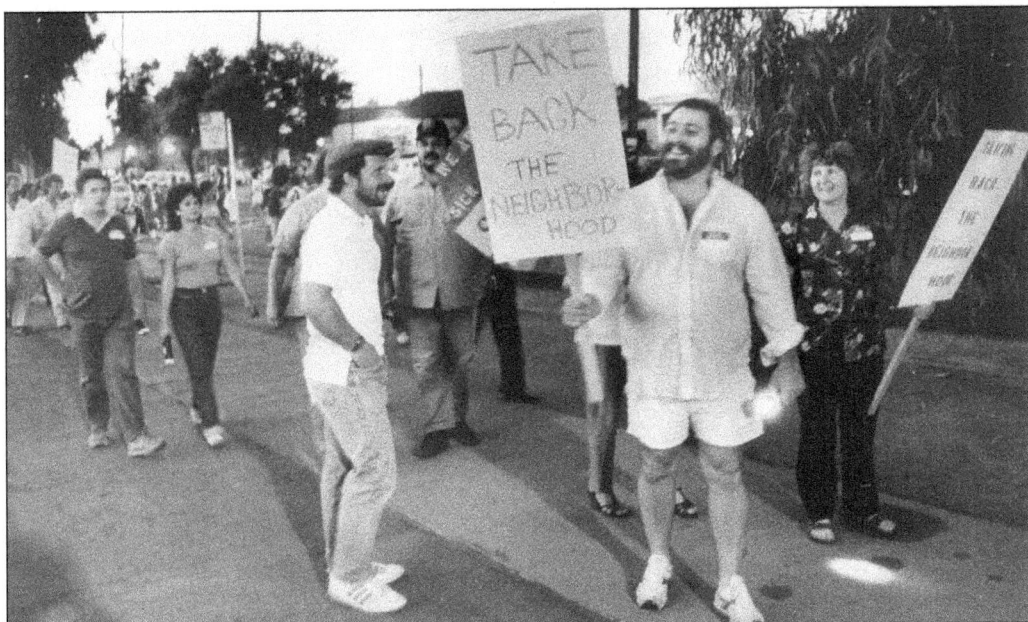

In this 1984 view, Dick Fisher holds a sign while marching along Stockton Boulevard with others to protest the criminal activity that had developed in the neighborhood during the 1970s and 1980s. The activists formed STOP (Sick and Tired of Prostitution) in an effort to rid the area of crime and vice. Businesses and residents continue their revitalization efforts to this day. (Courtesy *Sacramento Bee* Collection.)

The Coca Cola Bottling Company plant at 2200 Stockton Boulevard hasn't changed much since it opened at this new location in 1936. Nathan M. Sellers, who was the local distributor, poses with his 30 employees at the opening. Originally located at 3216 Sacramento Boulevard, the Sacramento City Council voted to permit the company to build a new and larger bottling works on the Stockton Boulevard site in 1931. (Courtesy Sacramento Valley Photographic Survey Collection.)

In this interior view of the Coca Cola Bottling Company plant, employees oversee the mechanized bottling process. During the 1930s, eight bottling companies were in operation in Sacramento employing more than 125 workers. These companies had more than $500,000 in assets and were bottling everything from mineral water and soft drinks to beer. Bottling at the Coca Cola plant continues to this day. (Courtesy City of Sacramento Collection.)

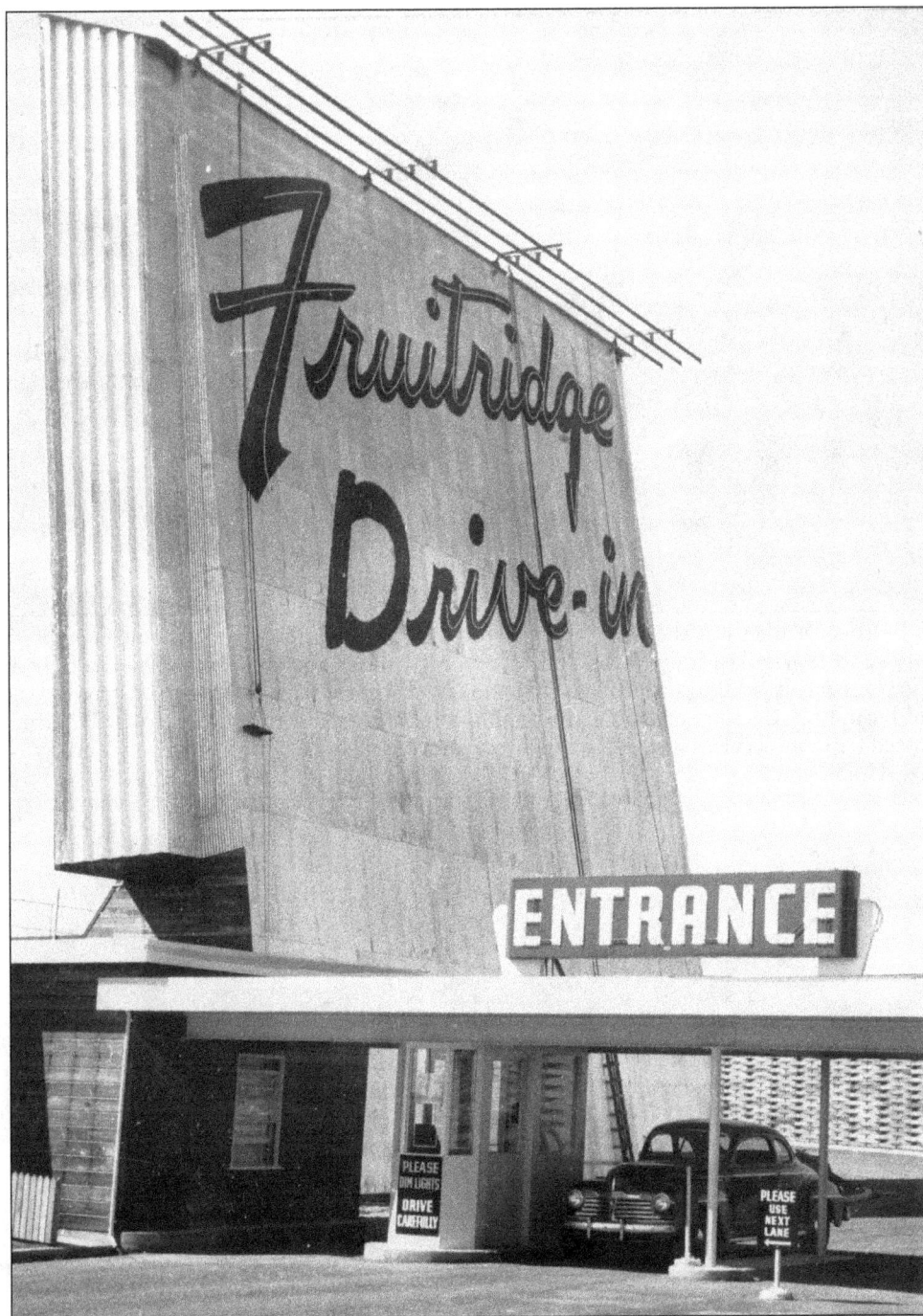

The opening of the newest drive-in theater in Sacramento was on June 17, 1950, at the corner of Fruitridge Road and Stockton Boulevard. The story in the *Sacramento Bee* noted that the theater was owned and operated by the Blumenfeld chain and that Paul David would manage the facility. Drive-in theaters were popular in California because of the mild year-round weather. Families would pile into their station wagons and enjoy an evening of entertainment. (Courtesy *Sacramento Bee* Collection.)

Inks Brothers Market was the first "anchor" store in the new Fruitridge Shopping Center when it opened in 1947 at Fruitridge Road and Stockton Boulevard in what was called the Fruitridge Manor District. In addition to the grocery, the center boasted a post office, theater, and other retail businesses. Sacramento County's population grew rapidly after World War II, bringing the need for more services to those suburban areas where families were settling. (Courtesy Noel LaDue Collection.)

The Manor Theater on Fruitridge Road, in the Fruitridge Shopping Center, was a typical tenant of the new strip malls popping up in all the suburbs around Sacramento in the 1950s. Playing at the theater in the fall of 1954 was the crime drama *Down Three Dark Streets* and the western *Bounty Hunter*. For the price of one ticket, moviegoers could see the double feature. (Courtesy Frank Christy Collection.)

Stephen Persic and Henry Brugger, recently returned from World War II, opened Perkins Lumber Company on Jackson Road near Folsom Boulevard in 1946. They operated what they called the "pa and pa" lumberyard for 46 years before large chain building supply stores forced the company to close its doors in 1992. Some of the outbuildings of the Perkins Lumber Company were once home to the old Washington Elementary School. (Courtesy *Sacramento Bee* Collection.)

Max Mueller and his family operated a blacksmith's shop on Jackson Road in the Perkins area of Sacramento County during the 1890s. Perkins Station was 5 miles east of Sacramento on the Southern Pacific Railroad line. It had a number of blacksmith shops, a hotel, meat market, saloon, dry-goods store, and post office. The Perkins businesses supported the nearby farms growing fruit, hops, and grapes. (Courtesy Sacramento Valley Photographic Survey Collection.)

Crowds watch as the Sacramento Box and Lumber Company at Sixty-fifth Street and Folsom Boulevard burned to the ground August 8, 1926. The loss was $200,000 and involved more than two million board feet of lumber. City fire crews stretched their water hoses across city boundary lines, because the box company didn't have an adequate water supply. Southern Pacific Railroad Company dispatched three water tank cars that helped save a portion of the lumber. (Courtesy Sacramento Valley Photographic Survey Collection.)

The Sacramento Box and Lumber Company rebuilt its operation after the fire at the same location. In this aerial view from about 1950, the Sixty-fifth Street Expressway is on the left and in the upper far left is the new California State University, Sacramento campus under construction. On the right in the background are the hop fields that eventually become part of the university campus. (Courtesy Harry Sweet Collection.)

With the advent of electrical power in California, a number of companies operated in Northern California. PG&E would purchase these companies and among them was the Great Western Power Company of California. At Folsom Boulevard and Power Inn Road sits the Brighton Substation. In the foreground are the original tracks for the Sacramento Valley Railroad. Today the light rail runs along the same right-of-way to Folsom. (Courtesy Laura Landrus Collection.)

The houses that appear in front of the Brighton Substation in this view are no longer there. The station has expanded over the years and now there are more transformers on the site. Power Inn Road (formerly Power Line Road or the Brighton-Florin Road) is on the right. Note that even though PG&E owned the station, the Great Western Power Company name is still on the building. (Courtesy Laura Landrus Collection.)

Proctor and Gamble built a plant in Sacramento County in 1953, bringing hundreds of jobs to the area. Situated in an industrial area on the northeast corner of Fruitridge Road and Power Inn Road, the undeveloped land adjacent to the Western Pacific Railroad was an attractive asset to the company. The plant has been in continuous operation for more than 50 years. (Courtesy *Sacramento Bee* Collection.)

By 1963, just 10 years after opening, the Proctor and Gamble plant on Fruitridge Road was in full operation. While the company manufactures hundreds of everyday products, coconut oil is the major ingredient produced at the Sacramento plant and used in the many soaps and detergents familiar to most Americans. At the time, the land surrounding the plant remained undeveloped. (Courtesy *Sacramento Bee* Collection.)

This 1959 close-up view of the elaborate tangle of pipes and smoke stacks at the plant demonstrates just how complicated the processing equipment must be to produce the coconut oil necessary for the many products made by Proctor and Gamble. The Sacramento plant is one of two Proctor and Gamble chemical plants in the United States and is one of the largest producers of coconut oil in the world. (Courtesy *Sacramento Bee* Collection.)

After being in operation 30 years, the Proctor and Gamble Company upgraded and expanded their production at the Fruitridge Road site. Seen here in 1982, the truck driver is carefully maneuvering the 112-foot-tall distillation tower through the gates and onto the plant property. The new tower allowed the company to increase its production of the alcohol used in the manufacture of detergents and other products. (Courtesy *Sacramento Bee* Collection.)

Starting out as the Sacramento Signal Depot at its first site on the old state fairgrounds at Broadway and Stockton Boulevards, the U.S. Army Depot began construction on a headquarters building and four warehouses at its new location on Fruitridge and Florin-Perkins Roads at the close of World War II. The Depot, as it was called, repaired and maintained high-tech military hardware and electronic equipment. (Courtesy Sacramento Army Depot Collection.)

Changing the name from the Sacramento Signal Depot to the Sacramento Army Depot in 1962 was a result of an army-wide reorganization. Known as Building 150, the administration building was the headquarters for the more than 4,000 employees who worked at the depot during its heyday. Here is the scene of the monthly retreat ceremony in 1965. (Courtesy Sacramento Metropolitan Chamber of Commerce Collection.)

Occupying 485 acres of land, the Sacramento Army Depot continues to serve as an important part of Sacramento's economy. With the end of the cold war, the military began to downsize. The Base Realignment and Closure Commission (BRAC) slated the Depot for closure in 1991. By 1995, the City of Sacramento leased 370 acres (a portion of the Depot land) to Packard Bell in an effort to reenergize the area. (Courtesy James E. Henley Collection.)

Packard Bell established its world headquarters at the Sacramento Army Depot with 5,000 employees in August 1995. It was Packard Bell's only manufacturing plant in the United States. This image shows the computerized sorting system, the largest west of the Mississippi River. The system locates, sorts, and guides packages to their final destination anywhere in the world. (Courtesy Sacramento Metropolitan Chamber of Commerce Collection.)

At the height of the Vietnam War, the Sacramento Army Depot played a major role in supplying the troops in the field. In addition to its contributions to Sacramento's economy, the Depot participated in community-service projects. Among the most successful was Operation Santa Claus, a program that served thousands of area residents from 1948 through 1995. Begun by military families and Depot employee James Nelson, the program gathered food, clothing, and toys at Christmastime. (Courtesy James Nelson Collection.)

Five

RAILS TO ROADS
BY CARSON HENDRICKS

The Southern Pacific Railroad and the Central California Traction Company (CCTC), an electric railroad, both dominated transportation in this area of Sacramento for the first half of the 20th century. As automobiles became the major form of transportation, more and more land was given over to their use. Notable in the majority of these images are the ubiquitous overhead power lines and poles, a necessary eyesore, particularly for the electric streetcars that were a major form of transportation. Upper Stockton Road, later Stockton Boulevard (formerly Highway 99), was the main north-south route. Highway 99 was later rerouted to the west in an effort to decrease traffic on city streets. This 1913 photograph looks west on Folsom Boulevard from the Sixty-fifth Street underpass. The tracks in the foreground were owned by Southern Pacific; the floodgates were added in the 1930s. Folsom Boulevard was the major road to Folsom and points east. Highway 50 was originally on Folsom Boulevard, but it was rerouted in the late 1960s when the current highway was built. (Courtesy California Department of Transportation, © 1913.)

Taken around 1908, this photograph shows a stretch of Upper Stockton Road, south of the old state fairgrounds. The automobile in the image is an Elmore, possibly a tonneau model. In the background, note the horse-drawn cart. Stockton Road was well maintained as the major north-south route, and this image captures the transition between horse-drawn wagons and automobiles. (Courtesy Ralph Shaw Collection.)

This south-facing c. 1910 photograph shows the new stop at Stockton Boulevard and San Francisco Boulevard on the main line of the CCTC. It was also the first stop for the new Colonial Heights subdivision. Colonial Heights was developed by officers of the CCTC to take advantage of the new line and its interurban service. (Courtesy City of Sacramento Collection.)

In September 1912, San Francisco real estate agents Stine and Kendrick operated a booth at the California State Fair to sell farmland along the route of the new CCTC. In the previous year, the company sold 10,000 acres of land along the line to Stockton. During planning and construction, developers were able to buy land along the route for bargain prices. (Courtesy Sacramento Trust for Historic Preservation Collection.)

A large group of sailors marches in front of the state fairgrounds around 1920 along Stockton Boulevard. Part of the road is now paved. Note that there are three sets of rail tracks and a streetcar in the distance. This photograph was most likely taken on an opening day of the California State Fair. (Courtesy City of Sacramento Collection.)

A Southern Pacific train speeds along the tracks paralleling Power Inn Road on August 18, 1951. The structure in the background is the Polk over-crossing for the CCTC; the CCTC line ran farther east, turned south to Stockton, skirting the Southern Pacific. Acting competitively, CCTC charged 10¢ less for a ticket than did Southern Pacific when it opened in 1910. (Courtesy Eugene Hepting Collection.)

This September 1939 photograph shows the Elmhurst streetcar near the end of the line at Forty-eighth and U Streets, a few blocks from the old state fairgrounds. The horses indicate that the image was probably taken during the run of the fair. This portion of the line was abandoned later the same year. During this period, PG&E ran the streetcar system in Sacramento. (Courtesy Bob Blymyer Collection.)

Sacramento City Lines car No. 92 travels along what is now Twenty-first Avenue around 1920. This was the private right-of-way for the CCTC. National City Lines (NCL) took over the streetcar line after PG&E was forced out of the business, and NCL then renamed the operation. This photograph is thought to be east of Fifty-fifth Street and shows development following transportation lines. (Courtesy Brian Thompson Collection.)

At the corner of Stockton Boulevard and Second Avenue, Central California Traction Company car No. 91 makes the turn onto Second Avenue. The CCTC ran interurban passenger service from 1910 until 1933, losing money on the business for several years. PG&E then took over the streetcar line. The CCTC continued to run their freight service along Stockton Boulevard until 1966. This image was taken around 1930. (Courtesy Grant Hess Collection.)

Taken in front of the former state fairgrounds, this photograph shows two Sacramento City Line cars (formerly PG&E cars). For safety reasons, in 1925, the city required moving the double set of tracks to the side of the boulevard rather than them running down the center of the street. The CCTC freight track was moved to the center of the road. (Courtesy Brian Thompson Collection.)

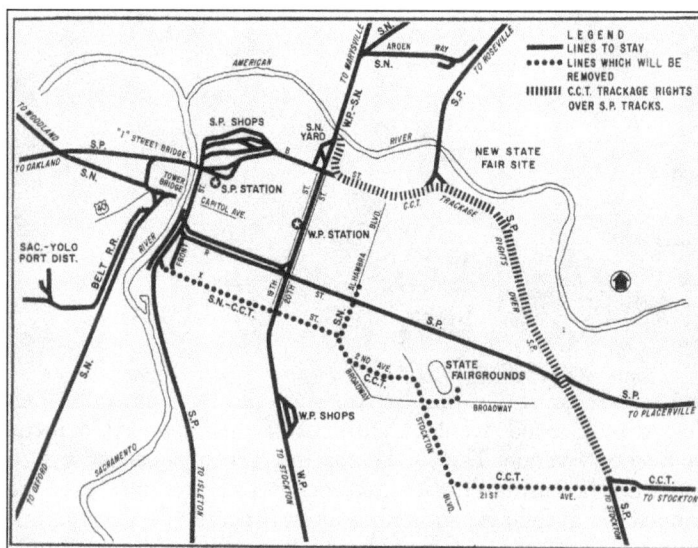

In 1966, the Interstate Commerce Commission gave permission for the CCTC to remove most of their tracks. This map from July of that year shows all of the tracks from Twenty-first Avenue, Stockton Boulevard, Second Avenue, Alhambra Boulevard, and X Street were slated for removal. This was done based on a petition from the four major railroad companies in Sacramento. (Courtesy *Sacramento Bee* Collection.)

In November 1966, the removal of the CCTC tracks along Twenty-first Avenue began. In this photograph, work crews manually load the heavy railroad ties onto a flatbed truck, while others are seen removing the rails from the ties. (Courtesy *Sacramento Bee* Collection.)

Evident in this January 21, 1968, photograph is the completion of the removal of the tracks along Twenty-first Avenue. The city considered plans to convert the center of the street into a parkway, similar to Elmhurst, along T Street. Soon after, the project was completed, and today the avenue has a park that spans almost the entire area between Stockton Boulevard to Power Inn Road. (Courtesy *Sacramento Bee* Collection.)

This rather desolate-looking site is the Standard Oil Company's yard on Stockton Boulevard at Thirty-fifth Street. Stockton Boulevard was the main north-south route, and this location was most likely a deliberate choice as transportation cost was an important factor in the success of the oil company's business. (Courtesy Arthur H. McCurdy Collection.)

Auto camps in the late 1910s and into the 1930s were ubiquitous in Sacramento. Graves Auto Camp, shown here in 1934, was located at the intersection of Folsom Boulevard and Elvas Avenue on the main route east of Sacramento. The City of Sacramento was supportive of the idea of providing sites for tourists and travelers by opening and maintaining a camp in McKinley Park. (Courtesy Sacramento Valley Photographic Survey Collection.)

Perkins Tire Service, at Jackson Highway and Folsom Boulevard, is photographed here by Eugene Hepting on February 15, 1954. It was previously a barn and livery stable in the former township of Brighton. Folsom Boulevard/Highway 50 had many barns, livery stables, and roadhouses, as it was the main artery east of the area. During the Gold Rush, it served as a wagon trail to the goldfields. (Courtesy Eugene Hepting Collection.)

This auto camp on Stockton Boulevard at T Street was located near where Highway 50 runs today and Highway 99 used to run. Like many others, it offered a range of services for travelers, including gasoline, cabins, food, and beverages. This photograph shows the improvements made along Stockton Boulevard by 1934. (Courtesy California Department of Transportation, © 1934.)

Taken in February 1944, this photograph shows Folsom Boulevard/Highway 50 east of the subway near Sixty-fifth Street. The handrail for the pedestrian sidewalk is visible in the lower left corner. By this time, the roadway had been greatly improved and had come a long way from its days as the major wagon road to the east. The Brighton Café and Campground is another example of an auto camp. (Courtesy Eugene Hepting Collection.)

Workers install floodgates on Folsom Boulevard between Sixty-fifth Street and Power Inn Road. They are preparing to apply caulking to the gates on April 16, 1935. The 1929 date on the retaining wall indicates when the wall was originally built. The gates were closed once for a test and are now inoperable. (Courtesy California Department of Transportation, © 1935.)

By 1950, Stockton Boulevard (formerly Highway 99) was handling large amounts of traffic as the main north-south highway. This view, looking south on Stockton Boulevard at the intersection with Fruitridge Road, shows how heavily traveled the road had become. As a result of increasing congestion, within 10 years construction had begun on the current Highway 99 route that bypassed this section of Stockton Boulevard. (Courtesy California Department of Transportation, © 1950.)

By 1958, traffic on Folsom Boulevard was heavy enough to justify a set of signals in an attempt to control traffic and increase safety at the subway. This view looks west on Folsom Boulevard toward the subway, with the pedestrian walkway visible. In 1962, the current route of Highway 50 was adopted and construction began a few years later. (Courtesy California Department of Transportation, © 1958.)

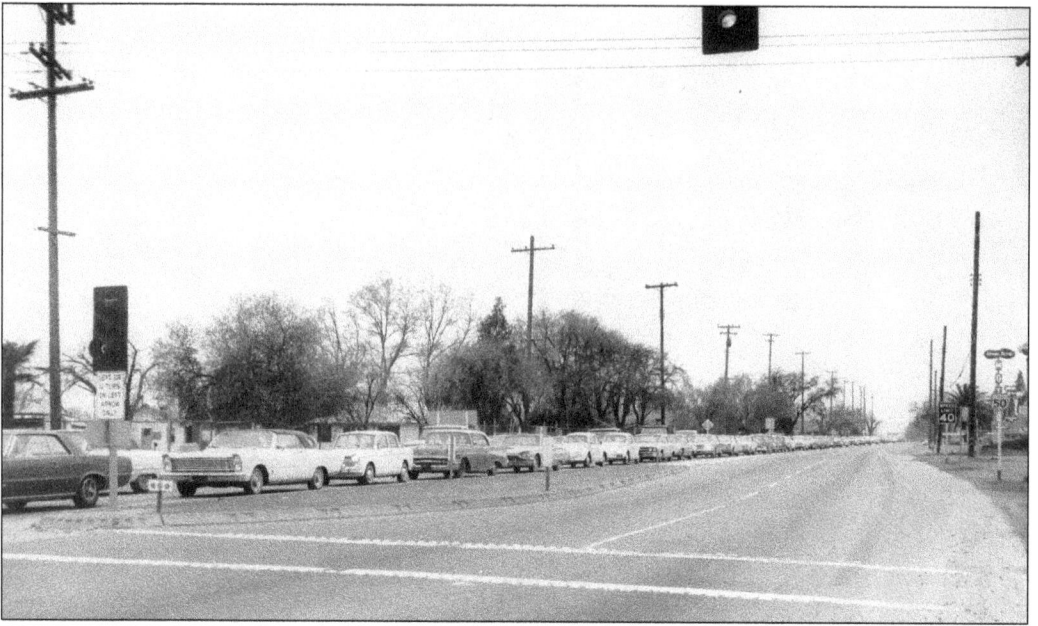

This image also looks west on Folsom Boulevard from Power Inn Road and shows heavy traffic in 1968. The new Highway 50 remains to be built, and this photograph shows how problematic traveling on this stretch of road had become. Today the intersection handles considerably more traffic than it did in 1968 and has also been widened and updated to accommodate the increased traffic. (Courtesy City of Sacramento Collection.)

Across Fruitridge Road from the Sacramento Army Depot, United Grocers built a warehouse and shipping operation to serve the many independent grocery stores in Northern California. This area continues to be an important warehouse and shipping hub given its proximity to major highways and train routes. The photograph was taken on May 29, 1961, not long after the site opened. (Courtesy McCurry Company Collection.)

On May 21, 1958, the California Department of Highways dedicated its research laboratory, located near Highway 50 and Fifty-ninth Street. The "Translab" is a world-class research facility for all aspects of highway construction. Many of the California standards set here for safety, materials, and construction techniques are used nationally and internationally. Several directors and staff have received international recognition. (Courtesy California Department of Transportation, © 1958.)

This photograph vividly shows how the current route of Highway 50 was carved out of the Elmhurst and Tahoe Park neighborhoods. Folsom Boulevard is at right, the SMUD building is in the center, and the old fairgrounds racetrack is at the upper left corner. This photograph was taken on March 19, 1971. (Courtesy California Department of Transportation, © 1971.)

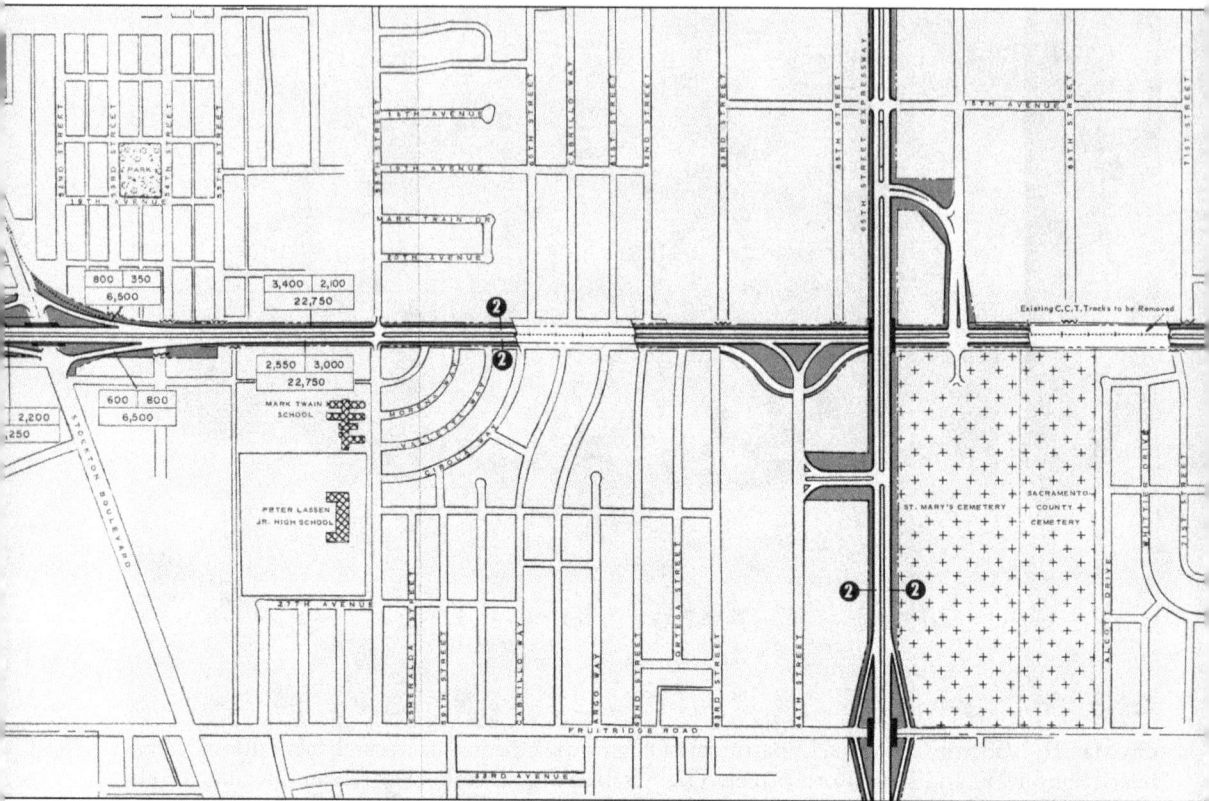

Highway construction can be difficult. On January 27, 1972, high winds blew down part of the scaffolding for an overpass during construction of Highway 50. There was no major damage, no one was injured, and construction continued on schedule. (Courtesy *Sacramento Bee* Collection.)

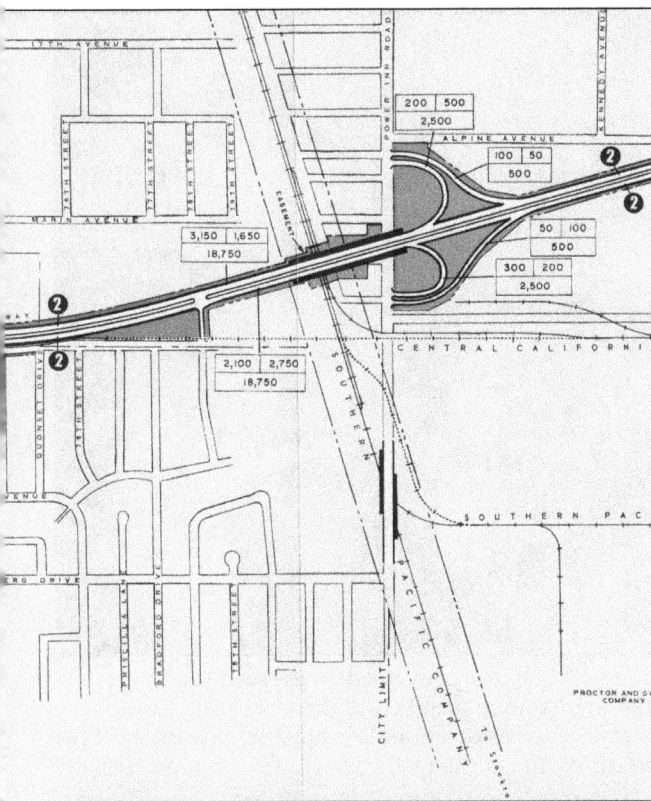

Done for the City and County of Sacramento, this plan is from the 1958 Trafficways report by De Leuw, Cather, and Company. This route, along Twenty-first Avenue, is one of several proposed highway routes. The report was significant as it presented a comprehensive plan for dealing with all forms of transportation, including removing nearly all of the CCTC tracks. (Courtesy City of Sacramento Collection.)

Highway construction can be difficult (part two). About eight months after the previous collapse, the scaffolding used for the concrete forms collapsed while workers were preparing to remove it. Ten persons were injured, but amazingly no one was killed. (Courtesy *Sacramento Bee* Collection.)

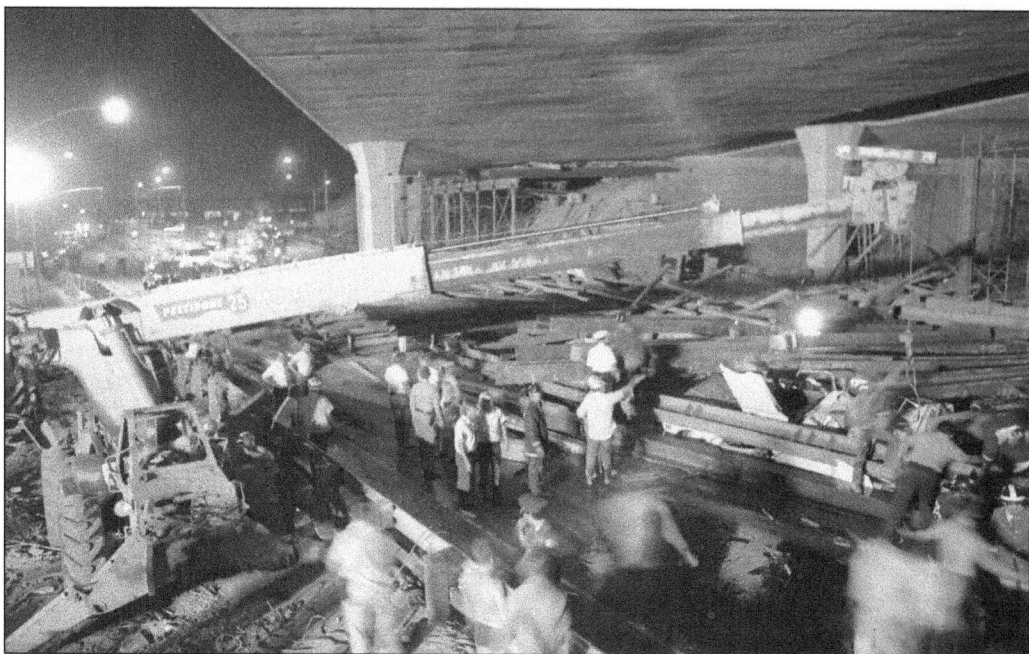

Rescue efforts at the collapse were large and swift. Dozens converged on the scene and were able to rescue all who were trapped. Most of the injured were members of the work crew. One of the workers, Glen Nelson, literally rode one of the beams down and escaped serious injury. This photograph clearly shows the scope and hectic nature of the rescue effort. (Courtesy *Sacramento Bee* Collection.)

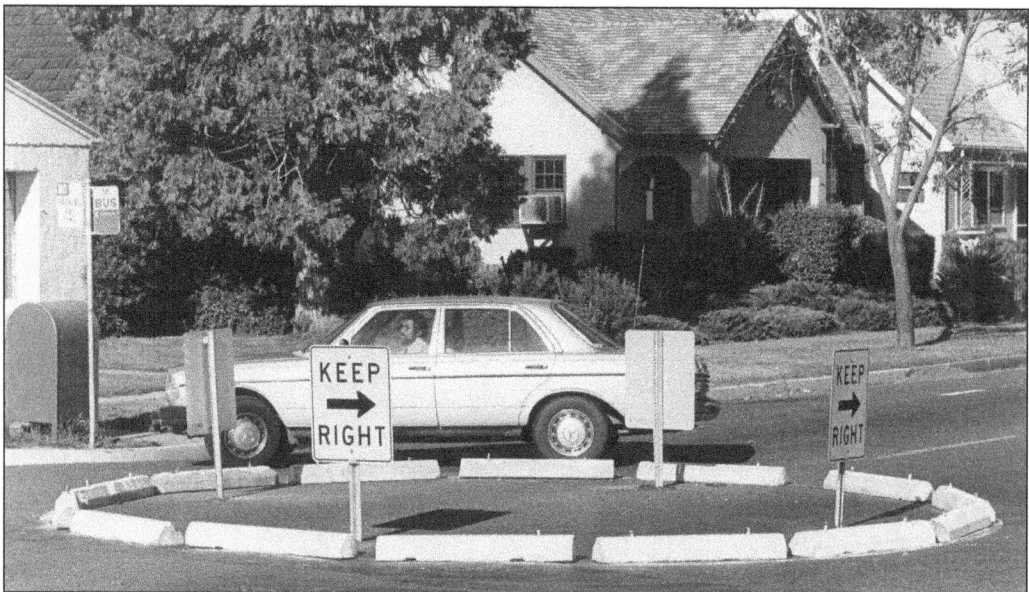

Traffic circles in Sacramento are not new. Responding to residents' complaints about speeding cars on T Street in Elmhurst, the city traffic engineer installed traffic circles at Forty-fifth, Forty-eighth, and Fifty-fifth Streets in 1980. They were temporary structures in the event residents did not like them. They were removed sometime later and replaced with four-way stop signs. (Courtesy *Sacramento Bee* Collection.)

Six

SACRAMENTO COUNTY HOSPITAL/ UCD MEDICAL CENTER
BY DYLAN J. MCDONALD

With Sacramento's rapid development and a steady flow of emigrants on their way to the goldfields, city leaders in the 1850s had to confront the issue of how to care for sick, injured, and indigent citizens. The maladies that disembarked on the city's waterfront— cholera, smallpox, dysentery, malaria, and yellow fever—were brought from all parts of the globe. The primitive frontier life and poor sanitary conditions the argonauts faced made catching an affliction more likely than ever striking it rich. The private medical care of the time proved too costly for most and city-run hospitals were generally inadequate. In 1869, the Sacramento County Board of Supervisors purchased 60 acres on Upper Stockton Road for $11,000 and authorized construction of a county hospital and poorhouse. Over the next 100 years, the hospital grew in size and scope, particularly after the 1960s when the institution became a teaching hospital in partnership with the University of California, Davis (UCD). This September 1947 aerial photograph shows the hospital grounds along Stockton Boulevard set amidst tree-lined neighborhoods and the California State Fair grounds. (Courtesy Joseph Benetti Collection.)

Completed in 1871, the new $80,000 County Hospital was designed by architect A. A. Bennett. The hospital, seen in the upper portion of this bond certificate, was four stories high, contained six wards, and had a library for patients and its own rooftop water tanks to supply its modern plumbing. Designed to care for over 200 patients, the facility unfortunately burned on October 5, 1878. (Courtesy Frank Christy Collection.)

As work on the replacement structure moved quickly ahead, patients were cared for at Agricultural Hall on Sixth and M Streets. The new hospital was built on the same grounds as its predecessor and designed by architect N. D. Goodell. The $65,000 two-story edifice had five wings (four wards and one dining hall) arranged around the main building in a spoke-like pattern. Completed in July 1879, it accommodated 150 beds. (Courtesy Joseph Benetti Collection.)

The Sacramento Society for Medical Improvement (SSMI) opposed the location of the hospital outside the city limits due its distance from the population the institution was designed to serve. Additionally, the society felt grouping the hospital with the poorhouse, while a noble effort, confused the two issues. The Sacramento County Board of Supervisors disagreed and moved forward with their efforts to combine both. (Courtesy Edwin Beach Collection.)

The rural location allowed for gardens, vineyards, orchards, pastures, and animal enclosures to be constructed on hospital grounds. Patients participated in raising food, caring for animals, and tending the grounds. The model for patient care, while saving the county money, proved difficult. How do the sick, infirm, or injured actually work to cover their medical costs, SSMI asked? This c. 1905 photograph captures the view from Stockton Boulevard. (Courtesy Arthur H. McCurdy Collection.)

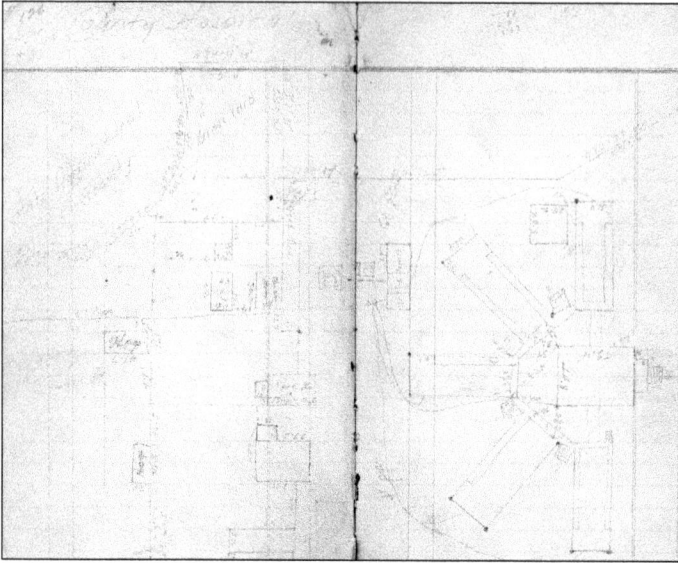

This 1905 survey of the property by J. C. Boyd, Sacramento County surveyor, shows the extent of the operations. Numerous outbuildings dot the map, including several sheds (wood, coal, and tool), a water tower, hog pens, and chicken coops. Note in the upper left corner of the drawing, next to the track of the State Agricultural Society (the old state fairgrounds), is a graveyard. (Courtesy Sacramento County Collection.)

In 1891, the county authorized the burial of indigent dead on hospital grounds; however, the first burials probably did not take place until 1897. The 2-acre plot, or potter's field, likely saw hundreds of burials during its use, the last interment taking place in 1927. With the expansion of the modern hospital in 2004, the remains of 72 individuals were reinterred at the county cemetery on Fruitridge Road. (Courtesy Junius Harris Collection.)

Those admitted to the hospital had to be too sick or infirm to care for themselves, without means of support, and a confirmed county resident (nonresidents in cases of accident or sudden disease could also receive care). A county physician was placed in charge of the care of the patients and the management of the hospital. This c. 1905 view includes some of the orchards cared for by patients. (Courtesy Arthur H. McCurdy Collection.)

Two "patients" are entertained by a young boy climbing on the hospital veranda around 1905. The day-to-day operations of the facility were overseen by the county physician and superintendent of the County Hospital. Prominent among them was Dr. George Amos White, who served nearly continuously from 1872 to 1904. White received medical training in New York City and Philadelphia, and was considered one of the state's foremost surgeons. (Courtesy Junius Harris Collection.)

The hospital's main entrance was decorated for a patriotic celebration in this c. 1910 photograph. The hospital underwent numerous investigations during its first 40 years by both the board of supervisors and by grand juries after complaints of mismanagement, unsanitary conditions, and patient neglect. These investigations usually resulted in policy changes, hiring of more staff, and increased audits, yet the complaints continued and problems persisted. (Courtesy Junius Harris Collection.)

The board of supervisors moved to professionalize the staff and create a modern facility to combat the continuing problems at the hospital. In October 1915, plans for a new, modern facility by architect R. A. Herold were adopted, and in 1918, a full-time superintendent and a staff system were instituted. The new campus complex was built in phases, with this new administration building being completed in 1928. (Courtesy Frank Christy Collection.)

During the influenza epidemic in 1918–1919, the hospital turned over two wards to the Red Cross for the care of those struck down by the illness. Some 4,500 Sacramentans contracted the disease, and over 500 ultimately succumbed to the Spanish Flu, many while being treated at the hospital. Later, in a continuation of their earlier mission, the agency received federal funds to feed, cloth, and shelter transient indigents during the Depression. (Courtesy *Sacramento Bee* Collection.)

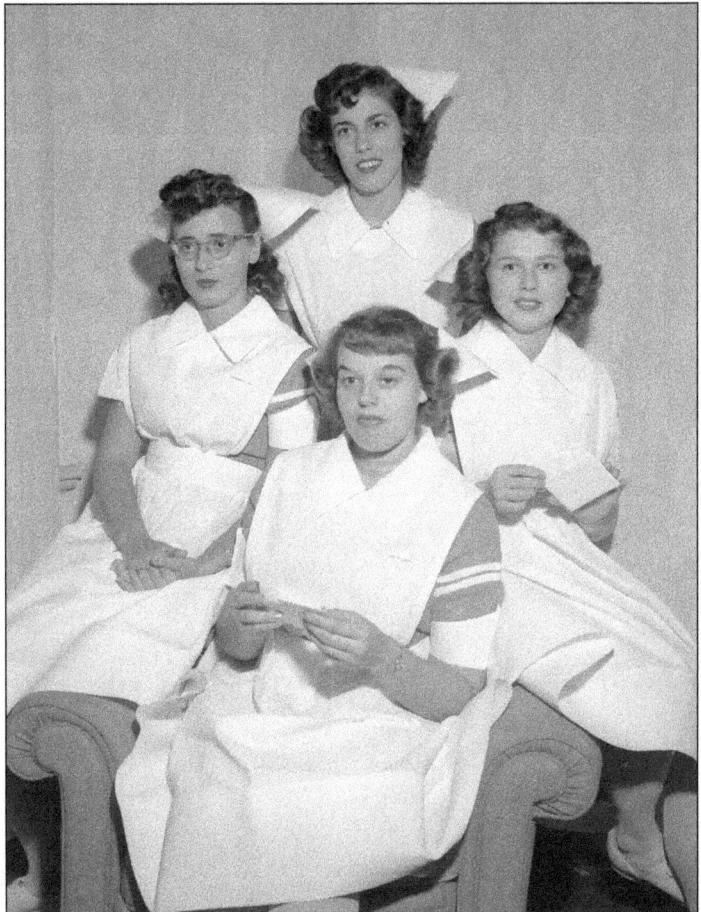

Civil service was adopted in 1937, and during World War II many of the staff served in the 51st Evacuation Hospital. The facility was designated as the polio center for Northern California, housing patients in Isolation Ward 21. Registered nurses, pictured clockwise from left to right, Rozanne Burzych, Elaine Stark, Frances Ellen, and Betty Peterson earned $235 to $286 a month by 1950 while working in the 800-bed hospital. (Courtesy *Sacramento Bee* Collection.)

After 20 years of little facility changes, new plans emerged in the late 1940s for $1 million expansion and modernization. The hospital superintendent, Dr. Leo Farrell, declared the revitalized hospital would be adequate for community needs "as modern as any in the state" and where "patients would no longer be sent home for lack of room." Early site work proceeds apace in this May 1950 photograph. (Courtesy Joseph Benetti Collection.)

The pavilion-style layout of the grounds, with each isolation ward connected by porches and tunnels, had not kept up with the rapid growth of Sacramento County. Architect George C. Sellon designed the new addition, the North/South Wing. Note the expanded footprint the new hospital would soon fill. (Courtesy *Sacramento Bee* Collection.)

This view taken in September 1951 documents the incorporation of the old building into the new. At right is the aged hospital; the old windows and roof are clearly visible through the second and third stories, respectively. The expansion raised the level of the old administration building from three stories to six and increased the square footage to approximately 140,000 square feet. (Courtesy Eugene Hepting Collection.)

By 1956, the new modern hospital had a staff of nearly 1,200, making it the largest agency in county government. Over half the employees were nurses. Patients were treated by 24 interns, eight junior residents, and three senior residents. County expenditures for the hospital totaled $4.9 million, with some $280,000 collected for services provided to patients who could pay. The pavilion style of the hospital was in use until 1964. (Courtesy *Sacramento Bee* Collection.)

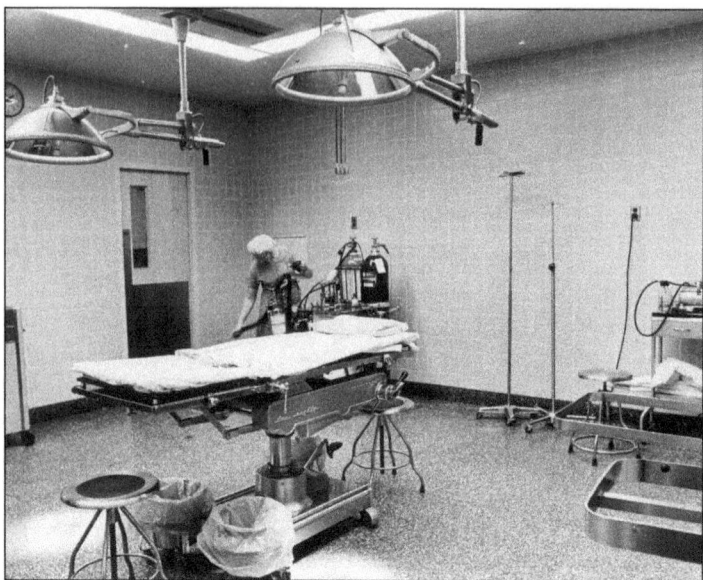

Workflow and transportation problems of the pavilion hospital led to a new four-year, $10.4-million expansion in 1964. The courtyard was filled with a new laundry/kitchen facility (34,000 square feet) and an eight-story Nursing Tower (120,000 square feet). Emerging technologies, as seen in this 1967 photograph of a new operating room, made the hospital amongst the most modern in Northern California. (Courtesy *Sacramento Bee* Collection.)

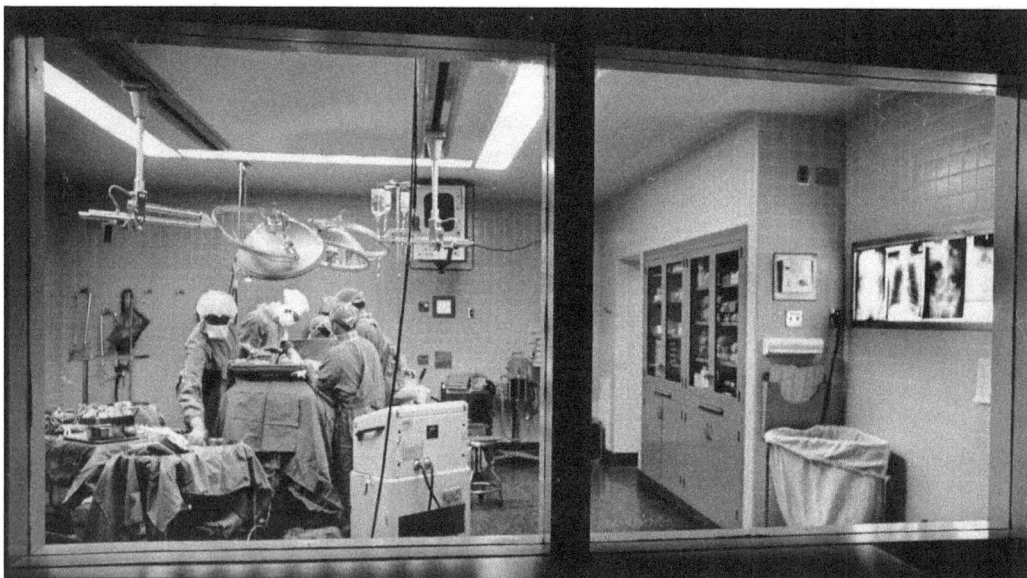

A surgical team carefully operates on a patient in May 1968 in the newly expanded facilities. Now a community hospital, meaning any resident of the Sacramento Valley was eligible for care, the facility began accepting Medi-Cal and Medicare patients in 1966. That year also saw the beginning of a transformative relationship with UCD, which planned to make the facility into a primary teaching hospital. (Courtesy *Sacramento Bee* Collection.)

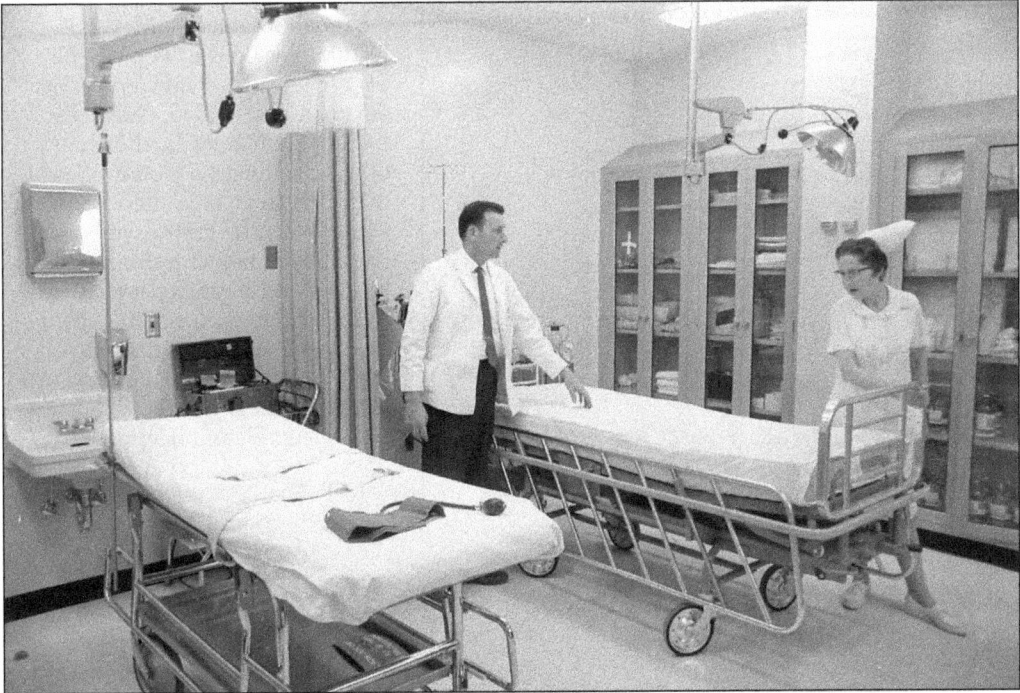

Dr. Edward Rapatz, director of Emergency Services, and Alice Johnston, head nurse, show off the new emergency department at the hospital that opened on April 22, 1968. UCD dean John Tupper moved to launch a new medical school as quickly as possible, and on September 23, 1968, the first 48 medical students took up residence. The hospital's mission now included education and research. (Courtesy *Sacramento Bee* Collection.)

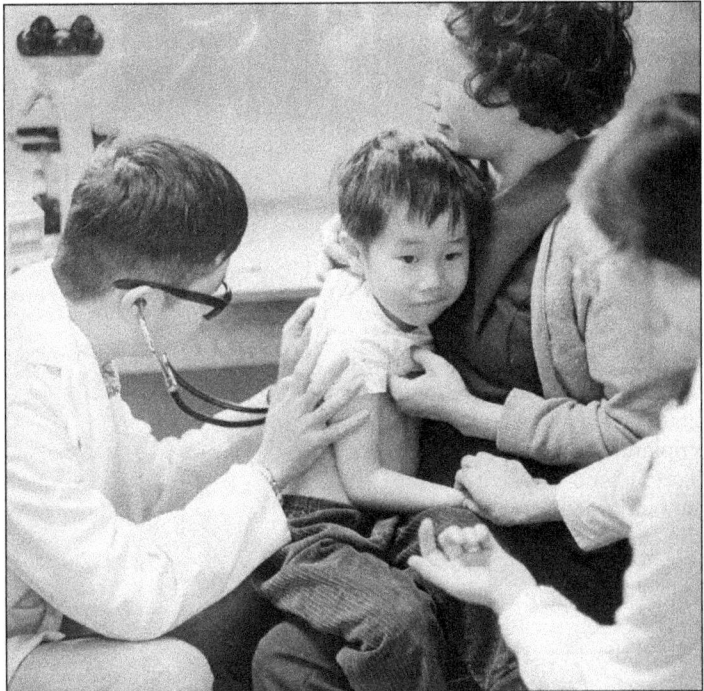

With its new affiliation, the Sacramento County Hospital changed its name to the Sacramento Medical Center in a ceremony on October 25, 1968. New funds and resources saw the center develop numerous programs, including in 1971 the area's first neonatal unit. Intensive care units focusing on infants and children allowed for multiple health-care professionals to work with critically ill patients and those needing after-surgery care. (Courtesy *Sacramento Bee* Collection.)

Chancellor James H. Meyer of UCD holds up the "key" to the Sacramento Medical Center during a July 1, 1973, ceremony. Joseph "Ted" Sheedy, the chair of the Sacramento County Board of Supervisors, presented Dr. Meyer with the key to symbolize the transfer of ownership of the hospital to the university. Exactly five years later, university regents changed the center's name to the University of California, Davis, Medical Center. (Courtesy *Sacramento Bee* Collection.)

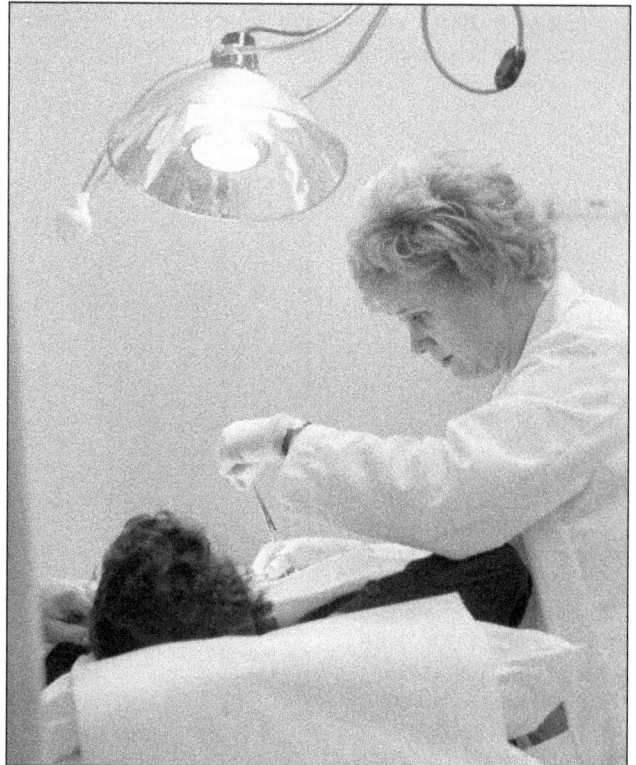

The hospital quickly became a pioneering institution by developing highly specialized research and treatment centers and by performing many complex medical procedures like heart and kidney transplants, pacemaker implants, and care of cancer patients and accident victims. To accommodate its growing needs, the center purchased 32 acres of the old fairgrounds for expansion. Dr. Jo Ann Hein treats a patient in the emergency room on Christmas Eve, 1973. (Courtesy *Sacramento Bee* Collection.)

By 1976, the center employed over 2,600 people, including 289 residents and interns, 252 medical-school faculty, 465 attending staff members, and 393 registered nurses. The 511-bed facility averaged 1,200 admissions and 3,800 emergency room visits a month. The operating budget of the nearly 700,000-square-foot facility totaled $46 million. Staff undergoes training during this mock air-disaster drill on December 4, 1975. (Courtesy *Sacramento Bee* Collection.)

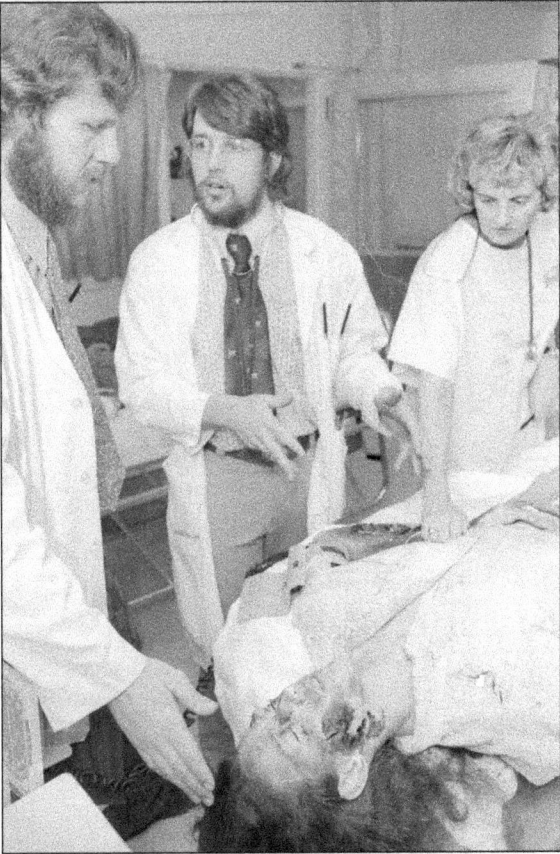

The medical center's Life Flight helicopter sits prepared for its next call *c.* 1994. Completion of Davis Tower in 1999 provided the emergency helicopter service with a new helipad. The hospital provides inland Northern California its only level one trauma center with comprehensive adult and pediatric emergency departments. Nearly 48,000 patients were treated by the department during the 2005–2006 fiscal year. (Courtesy City of Sacramento Collection.)

Today little physical traces of the old County Hospital remain and in its place a world-class teaching hospital stands. The medical center campus is spread over 141 acres and some 44 buildings. Staff number over 6,400 and operating expenses near $800 million. The dynamic hospital proves a vital community resource, something civic leaders hoped for when launching the venture during the city's tumultuous beginnings. (Courtesy City of Sacramento Collection.)

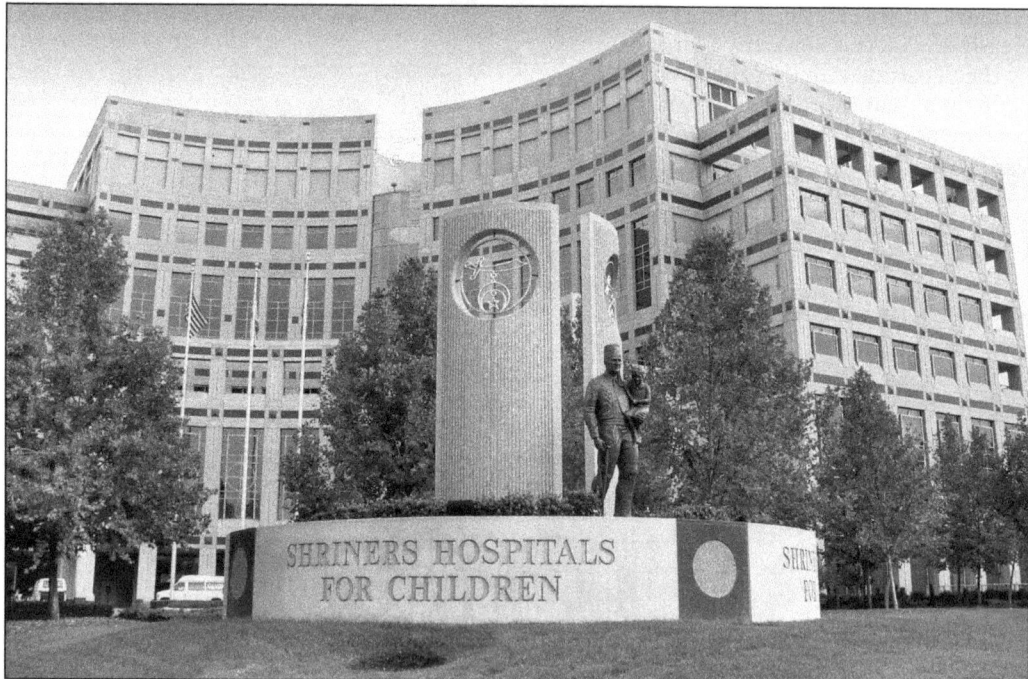

Opening on April 15, 1997, the 80-bed Shriners Hospitals for Children-Northern California offers care for children in three areas—spinal cord injuries, orthopaedics, and burns. One of 22 hospitals in the Shriners' system, the facility offers free medical care to children. Located in the Stockton Boulevard medical complex, just south of the UCD Medical Center, the two hospitals jointly fund the Institute for Pediatric Regenerative Medicine. (Courtesy Rob Jones Collection.)

Seven

CALIFORNIA STATE FAIR AND EXPOSITION
BY DYLAN J. MCDONALD

The state fair is a California institution, tracing its roots to the Gold Rush era. On May 13, 1854, the state legislature created the State Agricultural Society, authorized it to hold an exhibition, and provided $5,000 for the payment of premiums. Numerous interests around the state lobbied for creation of the society as a way to promote the state's abundant agricultural products. The first fair was held in San Francisco in 1854, with displays at Musical Hall and a livestock show at Mission Delores. Over the next few years, the fair was held in Sacramento, San Jose, Stockton, and Marysville before the legislature decreed in 1861 that Sacramento become the permanent home for the annual event. The fair was held at sites near the Capitol and in Boulevard Park during its early years. In 1909, the fair moved to a site on Stockton Boulevard and Broadway. One of the newly constructed structures, the Horticulture Building, seen here with families picnicking on the surrounding grounds, burned in 1916 (see page 125). (Courtesy Sacramento Trust for Historic Preservation Collection.)

Constructed in 1919, the Agriculture and Horticultural Building (later the Counties Exhibit Building), pictured here in August 1929, replaced the former structure destroyed by fire (see page 125). By 1954, the building boasted a 230-ton, 18-unit air-conditioning system, which provided fairgoers needed relief from the summer heat. Its striking architectural style and its position near the main gate made the building the focal point of the fair. (Courtesy McCurry Company Collection.)

The state legislature appropriated $30,000 to build Machinery Hall and another $10,000 for a water plant. Both structures were built in 1909. The hall provided exhibition space for California businesses to display their wares, while the water tower was needed to handle the increase in livestock exhibits. The tower, a landmark visible throughout the grounds, was razed in 1953. (Courtesy Sacramento Valley Photographic Survey Collection.)

Juried competition plays a central role in the state fair, bringing entrants from across the state. This drawing is the 1920 cover of the 248-page *California State Fair Premium List*. The rules and regulations, prize awards, and judging standards are spelled out within. Participants then competed in 19 different categories, in everything from animal husbandry to arts and crafts, for cash, trophy, and ribbon prizes. (Courtesy James E. Henley Collection.)

During the fair's anniversary in 1954, a time capsule, filled with a microfilmed survey of the last 100 years of California's life and people, was buried in front of the Counties Building. Constructed to last 20,000 years, the 3-foot-tall, 220-pound chrome and steel container is set to open in 2054. Gov. Goodwin Knight waves to the camera, welcoming the opening-day crowd. (Courtesy *Sacramento Bee* Collection.)

CALIFORNIA STATE FAIR 1920

SACRAMENTO Sept. 4TH–12TH.

CALIFORNIA STATE FAIR
SEPTEMBER 3 thru 13, 1953   SACRAMENTO

94TH OPENING
99TH YEAR

For the first time in the fair's history, all events were held in one location with one admission price. The Stockton Boulevard location also provided much needed room for expansion. By 1938, the fair was declared the largest in the United States. This 1953 map documents the numerous structures and activities at the bustling site as it neared its 100th birthday. (Courtesy Frank Christy Collection.)

Indeed, by the late 1940s fair officials began searching for a new setting for their event. This 1956 aerial view of much of the 207-acre site shows the urban development surrounding the fairgrounds, specifically Elmhurst to the north, Oak Park to the west, and Tahoe Park to the east. The numerous automobiles parked near the fair attests to the popularity of the event and the strain on its resources. (Courtesy *Sacramento Bee* Collection.)

Dubbed one of America's top attractions through the 1950s, and ranked amongst the top five fairs in the nation, the California State Fair featured numerous forms of entertainment. In its centennial year, a crowd gathers to watch country dancing in front of Agricultural Hall. Well-known entertainers who performed over the years at the fair included Bing Crosby, Lawrence Welk, Bob Hope, Peggy Lee, and Duke Ellington. (Courtesy *Sacramento Bee* Collection.)

The first state fair in 1854 drew 5,000 attendees; by the 1950s, it annually was attracting over 750,000 people. During its first 100 years over 15 million people visited the fair. Hosting the event was a great boon to the local economy, and Sacramento's civic and business leaders fought hard to keep the fair in town. Here crowds meander past Agricultural Hall in 1956. (Courtesy *Sacramento Bee* Collection.)

Large crowds could always be found in the grandstand when events were held at the fair's racetrack. Built in 1926 to replace the old wooden structure that had become a safety hazard, the new brick grandstand had seats for 7,000 spectators. This photograph was taken that September as the stock parade made its review before the spectators during Livestock Day. (Courtesy Eleanor McClatchy Collection.)

Aviator Charles K. Hamilton, the "Wizard of the Air," thrilled the crowds during his weeklong appearance in 1910. After mechanical problems and rough landings during previous performances, Hamilton finally pushed his 115-horsepower biplane beyond the mile-a-minute world record on September 9. The flight before a crowd of 20,000 ended in a crash at the three-quarter pole of the track, bruising the pilot. (Courtesy *Sacramento Bee* Collection.)

From at least 1913 to 1917, the fair staged spectacular locomotive collisions. The smashup was always a crowd pleaser, as this *c.* 1916 photograph indicates. The old retired steam engines, dubbed "California State Fair Specials," were sent hurtling down a 3,000-foot infield track. The event was well documented—note the numerous photographers in the infield attempting to capture the moment of impact. (Courtesy *Sacramento Bee* Collection.)

The sound of two battling locomotives crashing head-on at nearly 25 miles per hour was described as a "shattering, tearing noise," followed by several minutes of hissing steam. Afterward, about the only working parts were their bells. Due to lack of locomotives and a metal scarcity brought on by World War I, the spectacle came to an end after a crashing finale on September 14, 1917. (Courtesy *Sacramento Bee* Collection.)

These diving divas caused a stir during their exhibition at the 1914 fair. The *Sacramento Bee* said of the swimming and diving show, put on in two large tanks, that the "pretty water nymphs were attired in boy's bathing suits of the one-piece variety, such as have created sensations when first worn by society women at the fashionable watering places." (Courtesy *Sacramento Bee* Collection.)

Jimmy Lynch's Death Dodgers Auto Thrill Show had fairgoers on the edges of their seats watching the trick driving and stunt crashes in September 1954. The 30-act stunt show included jumping an automobile 75 feet from one ramp to another, driving on two wheels, and a contest to see which stunt driver could roll their vehicle the most times. Local television station KOVR provided a live broadcast of the event. (Courtesy *Sacramento Bee* Collection.)

Since its inception, horse racing has been a well-attended tradition at the fair, as documented by this image of a 1952 race. The state fair played a critical role in developing the sport in California. Local breeders like Nathan Coombs, Theodore Winters, and James Ben Ali Haggin all helped to develop the sport at the fair in the 1800s. Even when betting was outlawed at the fair from 1906 to 1933, racing still continued. (Courtesy *Sacramento Bee* Collection.)

This winning jockey in 1952 received more than a bouquet of flowers. The racetrack hosted other events besides Thoroughbred, quarter horse, and harness racing, including automobile, motorcycle, bicycle, and chariot racing; speedboat racing on an infield water course; water ski "carnivals;" tractor pulls; horse jumping; polo matches; wild west shows; firework displays; and evening performances by various bands and musicians. (Courtesy *Sacramento Bee* Collection.)

Demonstrating a horse and rider's skill, one of the West's oldest horse shows, dating back to 1903, calls the state fair home. Young Barbara Worth, dressed in her new riding habit, sits atop Waveland's Choice, a Kentucky-bred stallion, outside the fair's Horse Show entrance in September 1926. Fourteen-year-old Barbara lived in East Sacramento and went on to a career in training horses. (Courtesy McCurry Company Collection.)

The State Board of Agriculture reported on the vast improvement in the education of horses on display and the advancement in breeding at the 1914 Horse Show. By the 1920s, a larger area was needed for the show, but with the Depression and World War II, the proposed coliseum was postponed. Members of the Sacramento Riding Club participate in this publicity shot for the upcoming 1934 fair. (Courtesy McCurry Company Collection.)

The occasion to showcase California's agricultural, industrial, and artistic products lie at the heart of the state fair. Very few times in the fair's history was the show cancelled, and then only during wartime (World War II) or when larger celebrations took center stage (Panama-Pacific International Exposition in San Francisco in 1915). This August 1929 promotional photograph uses the fair's mascot to advertise for the upcoming exhibition. (Courtesy Eleanor McClatchy Collection.)

The state fair provides visitors abundant opportunities to interact with animals of all shapes and sizes. Besides the animal displays and petting zoos, one might find an animal performer on the Midway. Little two-and-a-half-year-old Cindy Mata hands Josephine, an organ grinder monkey, her nickel during her family's visit to the fair on September 2, 1967. (Courtesy Frank Christy Collection.)

The aggregation of all kinds of livestock—horses, cattle, swine, poultry, sheep, goats, and rabbits—for exhibition and judging at the California State Fair was amongst the largest in the country. Often entrants were turned away due to lack of adequate space to house and feed the animals during competition. Here a delighted crowd watches a sow suckle her newborn piglets at the 1952 fair. (Courtesy *Sacramento Bee* Collection.)

The mission of the state fair is to not only promote California products, but to also educate attendees about farm and animal life. The 1854 act founding the fair stipulated that the Agricultural Society establish "model or experimental farms" for educational purposes. This 1954 photograph shows a young girl feeding a fawn while other eager children press for a better view. (Courtesy *Sacramento Bee* Collection.)

Those who entered the juried exhibitions competed for various prizes. In 1920, over 2,100 head of livestock participated, making that year's fair the largest western livestock show ever. Premiums paid out then included $75 for a champion stallion, $35 for a champion bull, and $25 for a champion dairy cow. A hopeful dairy cattle entrant and her two attendants pose in this August 1929 photograph. (Courtesy David Joslyn Collection.)

Many juried entrants were children who belonged to their local high school's Future Farmers of America (FFA) organization or their local 4-H Club. They competed in livestock raising, farm mechanics, horticulture, woodworking, arts and crafts, and home economics. Displays of the winning entries, from floral arrangements to best comb honey hive, drew curious crowds. Here a judge's clerk reviews some of the 1952 ribbon winners. (Courtesy *Sacramento Bee* Collection.)

The Midway, with its countless sights, sounds, and smells, offered all fairgoers a thrill. Entertainment choices were abundant—a ride on the Ferris wheel or miniature roller coaster rides (seen with long lines in 1953), playing games of chance and skill to win a prize, and eye-opening sideshow performances. The take-home souvenirs and prizes from the carnival were reminders of the event's great amusement. (Courtesy *Sacramento Bee* Collection.)

Although gate admission into the fair in 1953 was 50¢, with children under 12 admitted for free, the carnival rides were priced separately. To appeal to the crowds, the rides were often painted bright colors, had flashing lights, and played calliope music. While their parents watched, these twin girls enjoy this centrifugal ride for children at the 1953 state fair. (Courtesy *Sacramento Bee* Collection.)

Performers on the Midway included this giant Uncle Sam, seen here in 1954 handing out candy. To produce a larger gate count, the fair held special days to attract certain groups, such as Farm Bureau Day, Woman's Day, Church Day, and State Employee's Day. It was not uncommon after World War II to have to close the gates after the fairground's capacity had been reached. (Courtesy *Sacramento Bee* Collection.)

A visit to the fair is not complete without sampling the smorgasbord of candies, finger foods, and stick meals offered by vendors and restaurants that included cinnamon rolls, scones, funnel cakes, corn dogs, watermelon, ice-cold lemonade, cotton candy, caramel apples, and fried chicken. Enjoying their meal during the 1953 fair are, from left to right, Mr. and Mrs. George Smith, Nancy McFarland, Carolee Powers, Mrs. Glen McFarland, Marilyn and Barbara McFarland, and Jennell Powers. (Courtesy *Sacramento Bee* Collection.)

A tour of the state in miniature, the Counties Building provided visitors with a broad overview of California county by county, as well as a place to beat the heat. Most of the state's 58 counties eagerly participated, giving each an opportunity to exhibit their locale's products, people, and history. Finishing touches on the displays are in motion in this August 26, 1958, *Sacramento Union* photograph. (Courtesy Frank Christy Collection.)

Besides the county's exhibit, seen in this 1954 image, crowds flocked to see the stunning arrangements in the Hall of Flowers, the craft work displays in the Women's Building, and the weaponry at the Armed Forces Exhibit. With over 60 buildings, many designed for children—including the Puppet Show, the Junior Museum, and the Kiddie Carnival—there was something for the whole family to enjoy. (Courtesy *Sacramento Bee* Collection.)

California businesses used the fair to showcase their various products. This September 1929 photograph of the interior of Machinery Hall captures the display of Sacramento's Crane Company, a plumbing and agricultural hardware dealer at Front and M Streets. Other industry and commerce exhibits were in the Home Show Building and the Foods and Hobbies Building, with everything from the latest farm machinery to new kitchen gadgets. (Courtesy Betty Jane Powell Collection.)

The fair lost several buildings to fires, including this September 3, 1916, event that destroyed the Horticulture Pavilion. The loss of the seven-year-old building and its exhibits totaled $200,000. The blaze occurred when chemicals from film developing ignited in the building's annex. The Agriculture and Horticultural Building (later the Counties Exhibit Building) would be built on the site in 1919. (Courtesy Sacramento Trust for Historic Preservation Collection.)

Throughout the fair's history, numerous gimmicky contests were staged for publicity purposes. On September 3, 1924, the family of Mr. and Mrs. Joseph Domingo were awarded an automobile for wining the "largest family in the state" contest. The Sacramento family consisted of eight boys and eight girls. In this ceremonial photograph at the racetrack, Gov. Friend Richardson presents Mr. Domingo with the prize. (Courtesy Frank Domingo Family Collection.)

Beauty pageants are also part of the competition at the fair. Young women from around the state, winners at the local and county level, vied to be crowned the next Maid of California. Contestants in the 1953 California State Fair and Exposition Queen pose in their best swimwear outside the Counties Building. Miss Barbara Lee Nutter (center) of Tulare was crowned the Maid of Magic that year. (Courtesy *Sacramento Bee* Collection.)

The success of the California State Fair and its growing needs required the state to begin searching for a new location. Negotiations began in 1949 for property along the American River adjacent to the North Sacramento Freeway (today's Capital City Freeway). The $850,000 deal finalized in 1950 for the 1,000-acre site. The fair bid a tearful good-bye to Stockton Boulevard after the 1967 exhibition. (Courtesy Frank Christy Collection.)

When the new California Exposition opened in 1968, visitors were greeted by old friends. Two of the golden bear statues, fixtures outside the Counties Building at the old fairgrounds since 1928, were moved in late August to places just inside the Expo's main gate. Once again family and friends could designate their meeting place by the statues, and the bear's vigil over fairgoers would continue. (Courtesy *Sacramento Bee* Collection.)

Visit us at
arcadiapublishing.com

www.ingramcontent.com/pod-product-compliance
Lightning Source LLC
Chambersburg PA
CBHW050548110426
42813CB00008B/2290